Chemistry Problems

Fourth Edition

David E. Newton

Adjunct Professor
University of San Francisco
San Francisco, CA

J. Weston Walch, Publisher
Portland, Maine

1 2 3 4 5 6 7 8 9 10

ISBN 0-8251-2413-1

J. Weston Walch, Publisher
P. O. Box 658 • Portland, Maine 04104-0658

Printed in the United States of America

Dedicated to

Rick Kimball

for many years of thoughtful and constructive help as editor and for being a good friend

Contents

Preface to the Fourth Edition

The first edition of *Chemistry Problems* appeared more than thirty years ago. The book was first written in response to an apparent need for additional practice problems in beginning chemistry courses. As a teacher of high school and college chemistry for nearly three decades, the author has felt that students require extensive practice in order to develop skills of nomenclature, formula writing, equation balancing, and the like.

Ongoing changes in the philosophy and practice of chemical education seem not to alter this fact of life. There appears to be a continuing need for a practice book that helps students develop these fundamental skills of chemistry. We are happy, therefore, to present this fourth edition of *Chemistry Problems.* Since the book first appeared, hundreds of thousands of high school and college chemistry students have used it to hone the verbal and mathematical skills required in mastering basic chemistry.

This edition includes a number of new problems dealing with acids and bases, molal solutions, electrochemistry, free energy, and Le Chatelier's Principle. In addition, we have provided an index to make it easier for you to locate problems and tables on specific topics. Finally, we have corrected some errors remaining from the third edition. Any errors found by users should be reported to the publisher.

David E. Newton

Exponential Notation

I. Express the following numbers using exponential notation:

1. 10,000
2. 0.0001
3. 10,000,000,000
4. 50,000
5. 2,000,000,000
6. 0.000 000 4
7. 0.0003
8. 790,000
9. 26,000,000,000,000
10. 0.000 000 045
11. 48,000,000
12. 0.000 000 000 000 000 001 3
13. 0.0175
14. 0.000 046 2
15. 3,000,000
16. 9,200,000
17. 371
18. 0.00900
19. 0.62
20. 0.000197
21. 328,500
22. 76,450
23. 0.9410
24. 3005
25. .000705
26. 80,000,000,000
27. 6240
28. 17,500,000
29. 0.05302
30. 0.000 000 000 009 15
31. 28
32. 7.480
33. 280,500,000
34. 134.2
35. 0.000089

II. Write the following numbers in the "long form":

1. 1.00×10^{5}
2. 1×10^{-12}
3. 4×10^{2}
4. 5×10^{-6}

(continued)

5. 3.2×10^{-2}
6. 7.95×10^{-1}
7. 6.854×10^{14}
8. 14.3×10^{2}
9. 9.065×10^{-4}
10. 4.3×10^{3}
11. 44.2×10^{7}
12. 3.08×10^{-3}
13. 16.9×10^{0}
14. 66.3×10^{4}
15. 4.00×10^{-6}

III. Carry out the following operations, using exponential notation:

1. 6000 x 0.004 =
2. 50 x 0.000 000 2 =
3. 800 ÷ 40 =
4. 4000 + 80 + 500 =
5. 30,000 x 450,000 =
6. 0.006 ÷ 0.2 =
7. 0.0002 x 0.04 =
8. 32,000 ÷ 400,000 =
9. 1,000,000 x 7900 =
10. 60,000 + 7000 + 80,000 =
11. 0.000 045 ÷ 0.009 =
12. 0.0024 x 20,000 =
13. 0.0064 ÷ 8000 =
14. 0.090 ÷ 0.000 03 =
15. 0.0004 x 5000 x 0.02 =
16. 450 + 250 + 7500 =
17. 400 ÷ 200,000 =
18. 6 ÷ 30,000 =
19. 90 x 0.02 x 0.000 01 =
20. 0.000 081 ÷ 90,000 =
21. 40,000,000 x 0.001 x 0.20 =
22. 300,000,000 ÷ 0.0006 =
23. 6450 + 28,200 + 3740 =
24. 0.060 x 20,000 x 0.0002 =
25. 4 ÷ 0.000 000 2 =
26. 13 x 0.000 001 x 4000 =
27. 4850 – 370 =
28. 0.006 x 0.0002 x 0.02 =
29. 0.0084 ÷ 42 =
30. 1400 x 2,000,000 x 0.004 =
31. 0.0045 + 0.0550 + 0.0015 =
32. 0.00072 ÷ 900,000 =
33. 0.0005 x 200 x 40,000,000 =
34. 0.049 – 0.00017 =

(continued)

35. $0.0002 \times 8000 \times 0.02 \times 2000 =$

36. $\frac{8{,}000{,}000 \times 140}{.04} =$

37. $\frac{640 \times 0.072 \times 4}{160{,}000 \times 0.00036} =$

38. $\frac{30}{60{,}000 \times 0.05} =$

39. $\frac{42 \times 0.00070}{0.35 \times 30{,}000 \times 140} =$

40. $\frac{450 \times 0.008 \times 0.02}{20{,}000 \times 40 \times 0.18} =$

41. $\frac{28{,}000 \times 0.0056}{0.00049 \times 16} =$

42. $\frac{240{,}000 \times 0.003}{0.00016} =$

43. $\frac{0.000\,035}{700 \times 0.001} =$

44. $\frac{32 \times 0.0007 \times 0.02}{20{,}000 \times 0.04 \times 70} =$

45. $\frac{150{,}000 \times 0.008 \times 200}{0.05 \times 160} =$

46. $\frac{400{,}000 \times 0.000\,003\,6}{30 \times 0.0000002 \times 1.2} =$

47. $\frac{420 \times 0.0090 \times 80 \times 0.0005}{200 \times 30{,}000 \times 3.6} =$

48. $\frac{350{,}000{,}000 \times 0.0064 \times 2400}{1.6 \times 0.000\,14 \times 36{,}000 \times 0.000\,005} =$

49. $\frac{0.9 \times 10{,}000 \times 450{,}000 \times 8.0}{0.005 \times 6000 \times 0.00072 \times 0.3} =$

50. $\frac{2.8 \times 0.000\,002\,5 \times 0.000\,000\,14}{0.0007 \times 50{,}000 \times 0.002 \times 210{,}000} =$

Significant Figures and Errors of Measurement

I. Determine the number of significant figures in each of the following numbers:

1. 5.432 g
2. 40.319 g
3. 146 cm^3
4. 3.285 cm
5. 0.189 lb
6. 429.3 g
7. 2873.0 cm^3
8. 99.9 mL
9. 0.000235 g
10. 144 lb
11. 2500 cm
12. 2500.0 cm
13. 1.04×10^{14} g
14. 3.58×10^{-9} nm
15. 48.57193 lb
16. 8365.6 g
17. 0.002300 mg
18. 7.500×10^{8} oz
19. 3.92×10^{-4} g
20. 1.000×10^{3} lb

II. Add:

1. 12 cm + 0.031 cm + 7.969 cm =
2. 0.085 cm + 0.062 cm + 0.14 cm =
3. 3.419 g + 3.912 g + 7.0518 g + 0.00013 g =
4. 30.5 g + 16.82 g + 41.07 g + 85.219 g =
5. 143.0 cm + 289.25 cm + 68.45 cm + 6.00 cm =
6. 29.49 cm + 83.46 cm + 107.05 cm + 26.618 cm =
7. 0.0653 g + 0.08538 g + 0.07654 g + 0.0432 g =
8. 1.8×10^{-5} cm + 3.25×10^{-4} cm + 4.6×10^{-5} cm =
9. 63.489 mL + 126.2 mL + 68.85 mL + 12.05 mL =
10. 2.3×10^{2} g + 4.62×10^{2} g + 3.852×10^{2} g =

III. Subtract:

1. 41.025 cm – 23.28 cm =
2. 289 g – 43.7 g =
3. 145.63 mL – 28.9 mL =
4. 62.47 g – 39.9 g =
5. 40.008 mL – 29.0941 mL =

IV. Multiply:

1. 2.89 cm x 4.01 cm =
2. 17.3 cm x 6.2 cm =
3. 3.08 m x 1.2 m =
4. 5.00 mm x 7.3216 mm =
5. 20.8 dm x 123.1 dm =
6. 5 cm x 5 cm =
7. 5.0 cm x 5 cm =
8. 5.0 cm x 5.0 cm =
9. 4.8×10^{2} m x 2.101×10^{3} m =
10. 9.13×10^{-4} cm x 1.2×10^{-3} cm =
11. 4.218 cm x 6.5 cm =
12. 150.0 m x 4.00 m =
13. 282.2 km x 3.0 km =
14. 14×10^{-8} m x 3.25×10^{-6} m =
15. 2.865×10^{4} m x 1.47×10^{3} m =

V. Divide:

1. 8.071 cm^2 ÷ 4.216 cm =
2. 109.3758 m^2 ÷ 5.813 m =
3. 24,789.4 km^2 ÷ 43.5 km =
4. 6.058 mm^2 ÷ 0.85 mm =
5. 4.819 cm^2 ÷ 9.852 cm =
6. 139.482 m^2 ÷ 68.75 m =
7. 4.23 m^2 ÷ 18.941 m =
8. 85.621 km^2 ÷ 8.05 km =
9. 6.023×10^{14} mm^2 ÷ 5.813×10^{12} mm =
10. 1.142×10^{-8} mm^2 ÷ 8.5×10^{-4} mm =

VI. Express the answers to the following problems using significant figures:

1. $0.057 \text{ mL} \times \frac{760 \text{ mm}}{740 \text{ mm}} \times \frac{273 \text{ K}}{250 \text{ K}} =$

2. $142.0 \text{ mL} \times \frac{745 \text{ mm}}{785 \text{ mm}} \times \frac{300.0 \text{ K}}{295 \text{ K}} =$

3. $51.3 \text{ g} \times \frac{44.962 \text{ amu}}{115.874 \text{ amu}} =$

4. $83.495 \text{ g} \times \frac{172.76 \text{ g}}{260.00 \text{ g}} =$

5. $6.025 \times 10^{14} \text{ cm}^3 \times \frac{20{,}000.0 \text{ mm}}{142.5 \text{ mm}} \times \frac{273.0 \text{ K}}{315.0 \text{ K}} =$

VII. Solve each of the following problems involving errors of measurement.

1. As the result of experimental work, a student finds the density of a liquid to be 0.1369 g/cm^3. The known density of that liquid is 0.1478 g/cm^3. What are the absolute and percent error of this student's work?

2. After heating a 10.00 g sample of potassium chlorate, a student obtains an amount of oxygen calculated to be 3.90 g. Theoretically, there should be 3.92 g of oxygen in this amount of potassium chlorate. What are the absolute and percent error in this experiment?

3. The melting point of potassium thiocyanate determined by a student in the laboratory turned out to be 174.5°C. The accepted value of this melting point is 173.2°C. What are the absolute and percent error in this experimental result?

4. A person attempting to lose weight on a diet weighed 175 lb on a bathroom scale at home. An hour later at the doctor's office, on a more accurate scale, this person's weight is recorded as 178 lb. Assuming that there was no real weight change in that hour, what are the absolute and percent error between these readings?

(continued)

5. The yield predicted from theory in a particular chemical reaction is 0.1062 g. The actual yield obtained by a chemist in a specific experiment is 0.0098 g. Calculate the absolute and percent error for this experiment.

6. A student decides it is possible to estimate the capacity of a test tube by treating it as a rectangle and neglecting its "roundness." On this basis, the student finds the capacity to be 100.5 mL. In fact, the real capacity of the test tube is 100.0 mL. What percent error has resulted from the student's neglecting the "roundness" of the test tube?

7. A chemist attempts to determine the surface tension of various detergent-containing liquids by using a tensiometer. In determining the accuracy of the instrument, the chemist tests the surface tension of pure water and obtains a value of 71.28 dynes/cm. The standard value for this quantity is 71.97 dynes/cm. What are the absolute and percent error of this tensiometer?

8. In an exercise to teach students how to use an analytical balance, the instructor gives a student a quarter which was pre-weighed as 5.6026 g. The weight that the student obtains for the same quarter is 5.6013 g. What are the absolute and percent error in this student's weighing?

9. The concentration determined for an unknown sample of hydrochloric acid by a student is 0.1355 N. According to the instructor's information, the true normality of this solution is 0.1364 N. What are the absolute and percent error in this titration?

10. An object with a pre-weighed mass of exactly (and correctly) 0.54 g is given to two students. One student obtains a weight of 0.59 g for the object, while another says the weight is 0.49 g. Which of the students, if either, has the greater percent error in this experiment?

11. In an experiment to determine the density of a liquid, an error of no more than 5.0% is permitted. The true value for this density is 1.4392 g/cm^3. What are the maximum and minimum values which a student may obtain to fall within the acceptable range?

12. An instructor has decided that students' weighing of a metal bar must lie within ± 2.5% of the bar's true mass of 84.556 g. What is the range of weights which will be accepted?

(continued)

13. What are the minimum and maximum possible values of the measurement 865.8 ± 0.4 cm?

14. What is the uncertainty of the result of adding 35.08 ± 0.02 g and 40.05 ± 0.01 g?

15. What is the uncertainty in the product of 350 ± 4 cm and 55 ± 3 cm?

16. What is the smallest number that could result from subtracting 22 ± 2 from 35 ± 3?

17. The dimensions of a rectangle are measured to be 20.0 ± 0.1 cm and 2.5 ± 0.1 cm. Express the area of the rectangle, including the uncertainty of the measurement.

18. 237.5 ± 0.01 g of a liquid have a volume of 1500 ± 5.0 cm^3. Calculate the density of this liquid, showing the uncertainty in the answer.

19. A chemist precipitates out a certain amount of a chemical into a crucible whose weight is 55.127 ± 0.001 g. After precipitation, the crucible and contents weigh 73.641 ± 0.001 g.

    a. Calculate the amount of precipitate formed.

    b. Calculate the uncertainty in this measurement.

20. In a particular experiment, the heat from a burning candle is used to raise the temperature of a volume of water. The results of the experiment show that 1.24 ± 0.02 g of the candle are consumed, while 430 ± 2.0 g of water has its temperature raised by 54.0 ± 0.2°C. What amount of heat was absorbed by the water? Indicate the uncertainty of your answer.

Dimensional Analysis

Use dimensional analysis to convert each of the following measurements to its equivalent in the units given.

1. 14 cm to meters
2. 31 g to milligrams
3. 116.5 m to kilometers
4. 285.9 cm to kilometers
5. 0.006394 km to centimeters
6. 8.4×10^{-6} kg to centigrams
7. 1.47×10^{5} mm to kilometers
8. 4.7 kg to pounds
9. 138.4 oz to grams
10. 65.5 km to miles
11. 23.6 ft to centimeters
12. 2.36×10^{4} s to days
13. 13.6 L to U.S. liquid quarts
14. 20.6 km/hr to miles per hour
15. 0.058 m/s to centimeters per second
16. 3.49 km/hr to meters per second
17. 14.7 g/cm^3 to pounds per cubic foot
18. 7.3×10^{-4} mL/s to cubic feet per day
19. 8.05×10^{5} g/cm^3 to kilograms per liter
20. 3.42×10^{3} lb/ft^2 to grams per square centimeter

Metric System

I. Convert the following measurements to milligrams:

1. 73 oz
2. 165.3 dg
3. 0.00238 g
4. 1.06 cg
5. 0.042 dag
6. 3.01×10^{-6} cg
7. 41.05 cg
8. 0.2 lb
9. 13.52 g
10. 4.6×10^{-4} g
11. 3.4 oz
12. 0.52 lb

II. Convert the following measurements to centigrams:

1. 938 mg
2. 19.3 g
3. 228 mg
4. 14.3 oz
5. 243.2 g
6. 0.28 dg
7. 8.5 dg
8. 0.31 kg
9. 6.3×10^{4} mg
10. 8.1 lb
11. 8.012×10^{14} μg
12. 4.2 hg

III. Convert the following measurements to decigrams:

1. 73.456 cg
2. 36.9 mg
3. 0.041 g
4. 1.52 g
5. 124.0 mg
6. 142.81 g
7. 0.895 kg
8. 23 cg
9. 73 oz
10. 238 μg

IV. Convert the following measurements to grams:

1. 41.5 cg
2. 3.89 lb
3. 0.9785 kg
4. 9.9 kg
5. 11.9 oz
6. 28.5 cg
7. 75.3 cg
8. 14.587 mg
9. 28.1 dg
10. 2.3 lb
11. 423 mg
12. 13.4 mg

V. Convert the following measurements to kilograms:

1. 2450 g
2. 147.2 hg
3. 89.9 g
4. 23.8 lb
5. 0.050 lb
6. 283 mg
7. 65.4 dag
8. 2.4×10^6 dg
9. 1.47×10^3 g
10. 6×10^{-4} mg

VI. Convert the following measurements to pounds:

1. 14 kg
2. 135.4 g
3. 71.9 mg
4. 5.1×10^4 g
5. 58.3 hg
6. 14.2 oz
7. 62 cg
8. 0.52 dg
9. 3.9 dag
10. 4.2 kg

VII. Convert the following measurements to ounces:

1. 23.7 g
2. 0.087 dg
3. 329 mg
4. 1.07 kg
5. 39.82 mg
6. 1.2 μg

(continued)

7. 4.3 lb
8. 46.5 cg
9. 3.0×10^4 g
10. 74.3 cg

VIII. Convert the following measurements to liters:

1. 182 mL
2. 3.4 liq qt
3. 4.2 liq qt
4. 0.895 kL
5. 135.4 mL
6. 750 mL
7. 22.9 cm^3
8. 43.2 mL
9. 158 mL
10. 28 mL
11. 60 liq qt
12. 250 cm^3

IX. Convert the following measurements to milliliters:

1. 14.2 L
2. 2.5901 L
3. 9.23×10^{-6} L
4. 7.20 liq qt
5. 0.323 L
6. 148 cm^3
7. 0.416 L
8. 4.38 L
9. 243 cm^3
10. 1.079×10^{-12} cm^3

X. Convert the following measurements to quarts (liquid, US):

1. 14.3 L
2. 254 cm^3
3. 70.5 L
4. 55.5 cm^3
5. 3.0 L
6. 386.9 L
7. 6.03×10^4 mL
8. 128 mL
9. 9.00 cm^3
10. 11.2 L

XI. Convert the following measurements to millimeters:

1. 16 μm
2. 85.4 cm
3. 4.32×10^{-8} m
4. 5.8×10^{-2} μm
5. 72.0 in
6. 125 μm
7. 234.5 km
8. 14.2 dm
9. 31.9 cm
10. 7.68 m
11. 6.0×10^{4} Å
12. 3.04 ft

XII. Convert the following measurements to centimeters:

1. 3.67 dm
2. 124 mm
3. 9.4 ft
4. 6.00 ft
5. 2.0×10^{4} mm
6. 36 dm
7. 11 in
8. 85.9 m
9. 0.85 m
10. 113 in
11. 7.4×10^{-5} m
12. 1047 Å

XIII. Convert the following measurements to decimeters:

1. 14.5 m
2. 5.15 mm
3. 57 m
4. 14.4 cm
5. 3.21×10^{11} μm
6. 1.4×10^{-4} cm
7. 106 in
8. 6.7×10^{-8} hm
9. 0.0628 mm
10. 42.0 in

XIV. Convert the following measurements to meters:

1. 1.0 mi
2. 1.0×10^{-9} mm
3. 78.5 cm
4. 39.0 dm
5. 1.00 in
6. 34.4 mm

(continued)

7. 0.468 km
8. 0.70 ft
9. 6808 Å
10. 0.99 hm

XV. Convert the following measurements to kilometers:

1. 23.896 cm
2. 562.0 in
3. 4.12×10^6 mm
4. 181 yd
5. 6.7 mi
6. 37.1×10^8 dm
7. 7.4 ft
8. 7.63 m
9. 0.023 cm
10. 43.5 m

XVI. Convert the following measurements to inches:

1. 245 mm
2. 0.438 m
3. 41.5 cm
4. 71.0 mm
5. 6.4 dm
6. 18.744 cm
7. 8.3 yd
8. 379 cm
9. 3.11 m
10. 2438 Å

XVII. Convert the following measurements to feet:

1. 5.67 m
2. 2.80 cm
3. 70.58 hm
4. 4.03×10^{-4} km
5. 5.07 m
6. 4.0 in
7. 31.43 dm
8. 6.21×10^8 μm
9. 67.3 mm
10. 121 cm

XVIII. Convert the following measurements to miles:

1. 13 km
2. 65.0 dm
3. 27.0 km
4. 3.06 cm
5. 28.9 m
6. 2180 ft
7. 413.3 yd
8. 745 hm
9. 0.051 km
10. 16.04 dam

XIX. Convert the following measurements to micrometers (microns):

1. 1.00 mm
2. 329. cm
3. 0.058 dm
4. 3.5 in
5. 11075 Å
6. 4.0 in
7. 4812.0 Å
8. 6.9×10^{-12} mm
9. 4.28×10^{-6} cm
10. 129 mm

XX. Change the following measurements to angstroms:

1. 63.4 mm
2. 6.4×10^{-6} cm
3. 4.017 cm
4. 1080.0 μm
5. 75.0 mm
6. 3.0×10^{8} μm
7. 1.00 in
8. 9.0×10^{-3} mm
9. 38.2 in
10. 111.1 μm

XXI. Convert the odd-numbered problems below to picograms, the even-numbered problems to nanograms.

1. 4.5 g
2. 0.0082 g
3. 0.065 mg
4. 3.17 mg
5. 2.9×10^{-4} g
6. 1.5×10^{-6} g

(continued)

7. 1.23×10^{-4} mg
8. 8.85×10^{-3} μg
9. 3.6×10^{-3} ng
10. 4.28×10^{5} pg
11. 28.6 ng
12. 153 pg

XXII. Solve the following problems:

1. A box having the dimensions, 14 cm by 8.0 cm by 3.0 cm is filled with water. What weight does this amount of water have?

2. A cylindrical tube has a volume of 30.0 mL. Its diameter is 3.0 cm. What is its height?

3. What are the dimensions of a cube holding 250.0 g of water?

4. A test tube is 13.0 cm long and 3.0 cm in diameter. What is its volume in milliliters?

5. Sixteen students each take 25 cm^3 of nitric acid from a stock bottle holding one liter of nitric acid. How much acid remains?

6. Determine the equivalent distance in the English system of the metric running distance of 400.0 m.

7. A service station attendant sells 1.5 L of gasoline to each of four chemistry students. If this gasoline was taken from a 50 gallon container, how much gasoline remains in the tank?

8. A long thin glass tube has an average internal diameter of 1.5×10^{-4} cm and a total length of 75 cm. What is the volume of this tube?

(continued)

9. A large river flows at the rate of 2.6 x 10^5 gal/sec into a boat lock 75 m long, 30.0 m wide, and 18 m high. How long before the lock will be filled with water? (1 cubic meter = 264 gal)

10. A micropipette holds a total volume of 0.10 cm^3. The length of the instrument is 25 cm. What is its internal diameter?

11. A large volumetric flask has essentially a spherical shape with a diameter of 12.5 cm. What is its exact volume?

12. The length and width of a battery jar are, respectively, 18 cm and 15 cm. If the jar holds 6.0 kg of water, what is the height of the jar?

13. Twelve samples of cupric sulfate, weighing 30.0 g each, are taken from a one pound bottle. How many grams of cupric sulfate are left?

14. A burette delivers 0.15 mL of water per second. How much time is required for the burette to transfer 18 g of water?

15. A one liter bottle of carbon tetrachloride is used to fill a number of vials containing one-eighth of a pint each. If 305 mL of carbon tetrachloride remain when all the vials are filled, how many vials were filled?

Energy

I. Convert each of the following temperature readings to its equivalent in degrees Celsius.

1. 32° F
2. 58° F
3. 5.8° F
4. 139.6° F
5. −42.4° F
6. −7.9° F
7. 273 K
8. 313 K
9. 330.4 K
10. 406.3 K
11. 134.7 K
12. 48.9 K

II. Convert each of the following temperature readings to its equivalent in degrees Fahrenheit.

1. 100° C
2. 0° C
3. 26° C
4. 175.4° C
5. −40.0° C
6. −155.3° C
7. 308 K
8. 361 K
9. 285.1 K
10. 196.4 K
11. 416.5 K
12. 89.3 K

III. Convert each of the following temperature readings to its equivalent in degrees Kelvin.

1. 10° C
2. 78° C
3. 35.4° C
4. 266.3° C
5. 159.5° C
6. −64.3° C
7. 17° F
8. 106.4° F
9. 63.7° F
10. 214.5° F
11. −38.7° F
12. −262.2° F

IV. Determine the amount of heat absorbed or released in each of the following changes.

1. 40.0 g of water heated from 10.0° C to 30.0° C.

2. 25.0 g of water cooled from 85.0° C to 40.0° C.

3. 65.5 g of water heated from 32.5° C to 48.7° C.

4. 135.6 g of water cooled from 95.8° C to 21.6° C.

5. 100.0 g of ice melted, with no temperature change.

6. 40.0 g of water, boiled at 100.0° C.

7. 30.0 g of aluminum heated from 15.0° C to 35.0° C.

8. 450.0 g of iron cooled from 125.0° C to 45.0° C.

9. 62.3 g of lead heated from 21.7° C to 136.4° C.

10. 195.4 g of magnesium cooled from 120.6° C to 14.9° C.

11. 1.5 kg of copper heated from 5.5° C to 132.0° C.

12. 47.8 g of lead melted, with no change in temperature.

13. 186.3 g of copper changed from liquid to solid state at its melting point.

14. The complete vaporization of 53.8 g of lead at its boiling point.

15. The condensation from vapor to liquid state of 235.5 g of copper at its boiling point.

16. The heating of a mixture of 5.8 g of lead and 6.2 g of copper from 5.8° C to 12.1° C.

(continued)

17. The heating of 125.6 g of ice from −165.8° C to −38.6° C.

18. The cooling of 145.5 g of steam from 382.5° C to 107.7° C.

19. The complete vaporization of 10.0 g of ice originally at −10.0° C.

20. The complete vaporization of 35.8 g of ice originally at −65.4° C.

V. Solve the following problems involving energy changes.

1. To change the temperature of a particular calorimeter and the water it contains by one degree Celsius requires 1550 cal. The combustion of 2.80 g of ethylene gas, C_2H_4, in the calorimeter causes a temperature rise of 21.4° C. From this information, find the heat of combustion, per mole, of ethylene.

2. Which of the following reactions are endothermic?

   a. $H_2 (g) + S (s) + 2O_2 (g) \rightleftharpoons H_2SO_4 (l)$ $\Delta H° = -193{,}910$ cal

   b. $3C (s) + 2Fe_2O_3 (s) + 110{,}800 \text{ cal} \rightleftharpoons 4Fe (s) + 3CO_2 (g)$

   c. $H_2O (l) \rightleftharpoons H_2 (g) + \frac{1}{2}O_2 (g)$ $\Delta H° = +68{,}320$ cal

   d. $C (s) + 2H_2 (g) \rightleftharpoons CH_4 (g) + 17{,}890 \text{ cal}$

3. The heat of fusion for ice is 80. Kcal/kg. How many calories would be needed to melt 7 mol of ice?

4. For a certain chemical reaction, at 400° K, $\Delta G = -17.6$ Kcal, and $\Delta H = -26.5$ Kcal. Find the entropy change for this process at this temperature.

5. Given:

   a. $Na (s) + \frac{1}{2}Cl_2 (g) \rightarrow NaCl (s)$ $\Delta H° = -98{,}230$ cal

   b. $H_2 (g) + S (s) + 2O_2 (g) \rightarrow H_2SO_4 (l)$ $\Delta H° = -193{,}910$ cal

(continued)

c. $2Na\ (s) + S\ (s) + 2O_2\ (g) \rightarrow Na_2SO_4\ (s)$ $\Delta H° = -330{,}500$ cal

d. $\frac{1}{2}H_2\ (g) + \frac{1}{2}Cl_2\ (g) \rightarrow HCl\ (g)$ $\Delta H° = -22{,}060$ cal

Find the heat of reaction of the following chemical change:

$2NaCl\ (s) + H_2SO_4\ (l) \rightarrow Na_2SO_4\ (s) + 2HCl\ (g)$

6. Calculate ΔH°_{25} for the reaction, and tell whether the reaction is exothermic or endothermic. Given the following values for ΔH°_{f}:

$Na\ (s) = 0$ $H_2\ (g) = 0$

$NaOH\ (s) = -102.0$ Kcal/mol $H_2O\ (l) = -68.3$ Kcal/mol

$2Na\ (s) + 2H_2O\ (l) \rightarrow 2\ NaOH\ (s) + H_2\ (g)$

7. How much heat energy is given off when one kilomole of hydrogen gas (H_2) at 25° C and 1 atmosphere is combined with enough oxygen (O_2) to make liquid water at 25° C?

8. Predict the heat of reaction for the following reaction:

$CO\ (g) + \frac{1}{2}O_2\ (g) \rightarrow CO_2\ (g)$

(Consult tables for any data required in this problem.)

9. Calculate the heat of combustion for the reaction in which ethane combines with oxygen to give carbon dioxide and water vapor. Data to which you may refer include the following:

$C_2H_6\ (g) \rightarrow 2C\ (s) + 3H_2\ (g)$ $\Delta H = 20.2$ Kcal

$C\ (s) + O_2\ (g) \rightarrow CO_2\ (g)$ $\Delta H = -94.0$ Kcal

$H_2 + \frac{1}{2}O_2\ (g) \rightarrow H_2O\ (g)$ $\Delta H = -57.8$ Kcal

10. Calculate the entropy change for (a) the melting of ice at 0° C and (b) the vaporization of water at 100° C.

11. What is the change in free energy at 25° C for the reaction in which hydrogen and carbon dioxide react to form water vapor and carbon monoxide?

12. Water gas (hydrogen and carbon monoxide) is formed when steam is passed over hot charcoal. Calculate the free energy for this reaction at 25° C.

Atomic Structure

I. Draw a labeled diagram of each of the following atoms. Show the number of protons, the number of neutrons, and the probable arrangement of electrons, as far as can be determined.

Z = atomic number

A = mass number

1. oxygen — Z 8, A 16
2. lithium — Z 3, A 7
3. calcium — Z 20, A 40
4. sulfur — Z 16, A 32
5. argon — Z 18, A 40
6. carbon — Z 6, A 12
7. potassium — Z 19, A 39
8. helium — Z 2, A 4
9. aluminum — Z 13, A 27
10. hydrogen — Z 1, A 1
11. beryllium — Z 4, A 9
12. fluorine — Z 9, A 19

(continued)

13. nitrogen Z 7 A 14

14. arsenic Z 33 A 75

15. bismuth Z 83 A 209

16. gold Z 79 A 197

17. ruthenium Z 44 A 101

18. platinum Z 78 A 195

19. cobalt Z 27 A 59

20. scandium Z 21 A 45

II. Write the electronic configuration found in each of the following atoms:

1. oxygen
2. chlorine
3. titanium
4. beryllium
5. cobalt
6. calcium
7. strontium
8. nickel
9. silicon
10. rubidium
11. aluminum
12. chromium
13. scandium
14. phosphorus
15. zinc
16. bromine
17. potassium
18. vanadium
19. gallium
20. selenium

III. Write the quantum numbers of all the electrons in the following atoms:

1. boron
2. fluorine
3. sodium
4. argon
5. oxygen
6. helium
7. potassium
8. hydrogen
9. magnesium
10. beryllium
11. lithium
12. carbon

IV. Draw diagrams to show how the following isotopes differ from each other:

1. hydrogen-1 and hydrogen-2
2. lithium-6 and lithium-7
3. boron-10 and boron-11
4. chlorine-35 and chlorine-37
5. argon-35, argon-38, and argon-40
6. germanium-70, germanium-72, germanium-73, germanium-74, and germanium-76

(continued)

7. uranium-234 and uranium-238

8. tellurium-122, tellurium-124, tellurium-126, and tellurium-128

9. xenon-129, xenon-130, xenon-131, xenon-132, xenon-134, and xenon-136

10. europium-151 and europium-153

V. Calculate the atomic mass of the elements listed in part IV. Assume the isotopic composition of each is as given below.

1. 99.985% ^{1}H; 0.015% ^{2}H
2. 7.42% ^{6}Li; 92.58% ^{7}Li
3. 19.78% ^{10}B; 80.22% ^{11}B
4. 75.53% ^{35}Cl; 24.47% ^{37}Cl
5. 0.337% ^{35}Ar; 0.063% ^{38}Ar; 99.60% ^{40}Ar
6. 20.52% ^{70}Ge; 27.43% ^{72}Ge; 7.76% ^{73}Ge; 36.54% ^{74}Ge; 7.76% ^{76}Ge
7. 0.70% ^{234}U; 99.30% ^{238}U
8. 0.089% ^{122}Te; 2.46% ^{124}Te; 5.48% ^{126}Te; 91.97% ^{128}Te
9. 28.44% ^{129}Xe; 4.08% ^{130}Xe; 21.18% ^{131}Xe; 26.89% ^{132}Xe; 10.44% ^{134}Xe; 9.01% ^{136}Xe
10. 47.82% ^{151}Eu; 52.18% ^{152}Eu

VI. Answer each of the following questions on atomic structure.

1. How many valence electrons does each of the following have?

   a. krypton
   b. arsenic
   c. lithium
   d. fluorine
   e. strontium
   f. silicon
   g. boron
   h. sulfur

2. Using the inert gas core convention, write the electronic configuration for the following.

   a. bismuth

   b. bismuth ion (Bi^{3+})

   c. xenon

   d. xenon ion (Xe^{-})

   e. rubidium

   f. rubidium ion (Rb^{+})

   g. manganese

   h. manganese ion (Mn^{7+})

3. What elements correspond to each of the following electronic configurations?

   a. $1s^2 2s^2 2p^3$

   b. $1s^2 2s^2$

   c. $1s^2 2s^2 2p^6 3s^2 3p^3$

   d. $1s^2 2s^2 2p^6 3s^2 3p^6 3d^5 4s^2$

   e. $1s^2 2s^2 2p^6 3s^2 3p^6 4s^1$

   f. $1s^2 2s^2 2p^6 3s^2 3p^6 3d^{10} 4s^2 4p^6 4d^2 5s^2$

   g. $1s^2 2s^2 2p^6 3s^2 3p^6 3d^{10} 4s^2 4p^6 4d^{10} 4f^5 5s^2 5p^6 6s^2$

   h. $1s^2 2s^2 2p^6 3s^2 3p^6 3d^{10} 4s^2 4p^4$

4. Write the electronic configuration for each of the following elements in the oxidation states given.

   a. Cu^0, Cu^{1+}, Cu^{2+}

   b. Al^0, Al^{3+}

   c. Cl^0, Cl^{1-}

   d. O^0, O^{2-}, O^{1-}

   e. S^0, S^{2+}, S^{4+}, S^{6+}, S^{2-}

   f. P^0, P^{5+}, P^{3+}, P^{3-}

5. Using the ((↑↓)) convention, draw the electronic configurations for each of the following.

   a. potassium

   b. helium

   c. beryllium ion (Be^{2+})

   d. nitrogen

(continued)

e. fluoride ion (F^-)

f. sulfur

g. silicon ion (Si^{4+})

h. neon

6. Write the Lewis electron-dot symbol for each of the following.

a. carbon

b. aluminum

c. boron

d. hydrogen

e. fluorine

f. neon

g. sodium

h. potassium ion (K^+)

i. sulfur ion (S^{2-})

j. magnesium ion (Mg^{2+})

k. boron ion (B^{3+})

l. argon ion (Ar^{1+})

7. Using the $\otimes$ convention, show the electron configuration in the lowest energy state of the following.

a. oxygen

b. boron

c. aluminum

d. calcium

e. sodium ion ((Na^+)

f. bromide ion (Br^-)

g. magnesium ion (Mg^{2+})

h. sulfide ion (S^{2-})

Bonding Reactions

Determine the type of bonding to be expected in each of the following cases. Then, use electron-dot symbols to show how the bonding takes place.

1. sodium and chlorine

2. potassium and fluorine

3. lithium and sulfur

4. carbon and hydrogen

5. beryllium and sulfur

6. magnesium and nitrogen

7. silicon and fluorine

(continued)

8. aluminum and nitrogen

9. carbon and chlorine

10. carbon and fluorine

11. sulfur and oxygen

12. germanium and hydrogen

13. calcium and chlorine

14. magnesium and phosphorus

15. zinc and bromine

Formulas and Nomenclature

I. Name the following compounds:

1. HCl
2. KOH
3. $HgOH$
4. KCl
5. $FeCl_3$
6. HNO_3
7. NH_4OH
8. Cu_2O
9. $Al_2(SO_4)_3$
10. N_2O_5
11. $NaOH$
12. CO_2
13. HF
14. $Pb(OH)_2$
15. NH_4NO_3
16. $NaHCO_3$
17. HgO
18. $Zn(NO_2)_2$
19. H_3PO_4
20. $CsOH$
21. Li_2O
22. $Ca(OH)_2$
23. $CaBr_2$
24. Fe_2O_3
25. H_2SO_4
26. $FeCO_3$
27. SO_3
28. $Ba(BrO_3)_2$
29. $Al(OH)_3$
30. $HClO_4$
31. $NaC_2H_3O_2$
32. Na_2SO_3
33. H_2CO_3
34. HFO_2
35. NH_4IO_3
36. LiH

(continued)

37. CO

38. $MgBr_2$

39. $SnBr_2$

40. N_2O

41. NH_4F

42. $AsCl_5$

43. $KHCO_3$

44. K_2O

45. Ba_3As_2

46. ZnO

47. $NaClO$

48. SrS

49. $Al(BrO_3)_3$

50. SbF_3

51. $Pd(CN)_2$

52. $ZnSiO_3$

53. $Mg(C_2H_3O_2)_2$

54. $Ca(MnO_4)_2$

55. $Be(NO_3)_2$

56. $NiSeO_4$

57. $RaBr_2$

58. $NaMnO_4$

59. PbI_2

60. CaS

61. Bi_2Te_3

62. $KClO_4$

63. $HgBr_2$

64. $CoSi$

65. P_3N_5

66. $CuSO_3$

67. $FePO_4$

68. $PbTe$

69. $HgNO_3$

70. K_2SiO_3

71. $AgC_2H_3O_2$

72. TeI_4

73. $Zn_3(PO_4)_2$

74. Ag_2S

75. $Cd(HCO_3)_2$

76. ZnF_2

(continued)

77. H_2SO_3
78. $Ba(OH)_2$
79. PbS
80. NaH_2PO_4
81. $NH_4C_2H_3O_2$
82. Ag_3N
83. SiI_4
84. $ZnCO_3$
85. H_3PO_3
86. SnI_4
87. $Pb(NO_3)_2$
88. NaF
89. $KAl(SO_4)_2$
90. KUO_4
91. $SmCl_3$
92. K_2S_5
93. $Fe_3[Fe(CN)_6]_2$
94. $PtCl_2$
95. PtI_4
96. NI_3
97. $MoCl_5$
98. $La(NO_3)_3$
99. Dy_2O_3
100. V_2O_5

II. Write the correct formula for each of the following compounds:

1. sulfuric acid
2. sodium hydroxide
3. sodium bromide
4. barium hydroxide
5. calcium oxide
6. hydrosulfuric acid
7. lithium sulfate
8. carbon monoxide

(continued)

9. manganese dioxide
10. sulfur dioxide
11. iron (II) sulfate
12. hypochlorous acid
13. potassium permanganate
14. silver chloride
15. copper (II) hydroxide
16. ammonium sulfide
17. nickel bromide
18. iron (II) oxide
19. bromic acid
20. ammonium bisulfate
21. mercury (I) sulfate
22. iron (III) oxide
23. magnesium phosphate
24. nickel bicarbonate
25. zinc hydroxide
26. hydriodic acid
27. diphosphorus pentoxide
28. aluminum phosphate
29. hydrogen acetate
30. copper (II) nitrite
31. nitrogen dioxide
32. phosphorus trichloride
33. sodium phosphate
34. potassium carbonate
35. phosphoric acid
36. lead (IV) chloride
37. tin (II) bromide
38. ammonium hydroxide
39. periodic acid
40. iron (II) hydroxide
41. carbon dioxide
42. dinitrogen pentoxide
43. silver oxide
44. aluminum nitride
45. manganese (II) hydroxide
46. ammonium carbonate
47. aluminum oxide
48. antimony pentasulfide

(continued)

49. barium carbonate
50. calcium phosphate
51. cesium carbonate
52. potassium silicate
53. silver chromate
54. magnesium sulfite
55. chromium (III) phosphide
56. cobalt (III) nitrate
57. zinc iodide
58. iron (II) fluoride
59. nickel (II) selenide
60. sodium bisulphate
61. lithium oxide
62. copper (I) carbonate
63. strontium carbonate
64. mercury (I) sulfate
65. potassium dichromate
66. manganese (II) oxide
67. nickel (II) chloride
68. lead (II) acetate
69. mercury (II) nitride
70. lead (II) hydroxide
71. tin (IV) chloride
72. selenium tetrafluoride
73. phosphorus pentabromide
74. mercury (I) iodate
75. iron (III) sulfate
76. nickel (II) sulfate
77. silicon dioxide
78. lithium phosphate
79. potassium antimonide
80. nitric acid
81. magnesium nitride
82. cadmium nitrite
83. zinc acetate
84. hydrogen nitrite
85. strontium hydroxide
86. lead (II) sulfate
87. aluminum bisulphate
88. disodium hydrogen phosphate

(continued)

89. ammonium aluminum sulphate
90. copper (II) sulfate pentahydrate
91. lead (II) nitrate
92. gold (III) chloride
93. tin (II) hydroxide
94. hydrogen carbonate
95. ammonium bromate
96. scandium bromide
97. bromine iodide
98. rubidium carbonate
99. potassium thiosulfate
100. potassium arsenate
101. silver potassium cyanide
102. sodium cyanate
103. permanganic acid
104. osmium tetrachloride
105. lanthanum oxide
106. germanium tetrachloride
107. erbium acetate
108. ytterbium oxide
109. calcium hydride
110. iron (II) ferricyanide

Equations

Write a balanced chemical equation to represent each of the following chemical reactions:

1. iron + sulfur → iron (II) sulfide

2. zinc + cupric sulfate → zinc sulfate + copper

3. silver nitrate + sodium bromide → sodium nitrate + silver bromide

4. potassium chlorate (heated) → potassium chloride + oxygen

5. water (electricity) → hydrogen + oxygen

6. mercury (II) oxide (heated) → mercury + oxygen

7. potassium iodide + lead (II) nitrate → lead (II) iodide + potassium nitrate

8. aluminum + oxygen → aluminum oxide

9. magnesium chloride + ammonium nitrate → magnesium nitrate + ammonium chloride

10. iron (III) chloride + ammonium hydroxide → iron (III) hydroxide + ammonium chloride

11. sodium peroxide + water → sodium hydroxide + oxygen

12. iron (III) oxide + carbon → iron + carbon monoxide

13. iron + water → hydrogen + iron (III) oxide

14. iron (III) chloride + potassium hydroxide → potassium chloride + iron (III) hydroxide

15. aluminum + sulfuric acid → aluminum sulfate + hydrogen

(continued)

16. sodium carbonate + calcium hydroxide → sodium hydroxide + calcium carbonate

17. carbon dioxide + water → carbonic acid

18. phosphorus + oxygen → phosphorus pentoxide

19. sodium + water → sodium hydroxide + hydrogen

20. zinc + sulfuric acid → zinc sulfate + hydrogen

21. aluminum sulfate + calcium hydroxide → aluminum hydroxide + calcium sulfate

22. calcium oxide + water → calcium hydroxide

23. iron + copper (I) nitrate → iron (II) nitrate + copper

24. iron (II) sulfide + hydrochloric acid → hydrogen sulfide + iron (II) chloride

25. potassium oxide + water → potassium hydroxide

26. ammonium sulfide + lead (II) nitrate → ammonium nitrate + lead (II) sulfide

27. mercury (II) hydroxide + phosphoric acid → mercury (II) phosphate + water

28. potassium hydroxide + phosphoric acid → potassium phosphate + water

29. calcium chloride + nitric acid → calcium nitrate + hydrochloric acid

30. potassium carbonate + barium chloride → potassium chloride + barium carbonate

31. magnesium hydroxide + sulfuric acid → magnesium sulfate + water

32. sulfur dioxide + water → sulfurous acid

(continued)

33. sodium carbonate + hydrochloric acid → sodium chloride + water + carbon dioxide

34. magnesium + nitric acid → magnesium nitrate + hydrogen

35. aluminum + iron (III) oxide → aluminum oxide + iron

36. potassium phosphate + magnesium chloride → magnesium phosphate + potassium chloride

37. ammonia + oxygen → nitrogen + water

38. calcium carbonate (heated) → calcium oxide + carbon dioxide

39. sodium chloride + sulfuric acid → sodium sulfate + hydrochloric acid

40. fluorine + sodium hydroxide → sodium fluoride + oxygen + water

41. magnesium nitrate + calcium iodide → calcium nitrate + magnesium iodide

42. aluminum sulfate + ammonium bromide → aluminum bromide + ammonium sulfate

43. potassium fluoride + barium bromide → barium fluoride + potassium bromide

44. copper (II) nitrate + ammonium hydroxide → copper (II) hydroxide + ammonium nitrate

45. sodium nitrate (heated) → sodium nitrite + oxygen

46. lead (II) hydroxide (heated) → lead (II) monoxide + water

47. ammonia + sulfuric acid → ammonium sulfate

48. hydrochloric acid + ammonia → ammonium chloride

49. copper (II) sulfate + iron → iron (II) sulfate + copper

(continued)

50. aluminum + hydrochloric acid → aluminum chloride + hydrogen

51. carbon + oxygen → carbon dioxide

52. calcium bicarbonate + calcium hydroxide → calcium carbonate + water

53. hydrogen sulfide + oxygen → water + sulfur

54. sodium hydroxide + calcium nitrate → sodium nitrate + calcium hydroxide

55. potassium iodide + chlorine → potassium chloride + iodine

56. sulfuric acid + potassium hydroxide → potassium sulfate + water

57. carbon dioxide + carbon → carbon monoxide

58. calcium sulfate + sodium carbonate → calcium carbonate + sodium sulfate

59. water + diphosphorus pentoxide → phosphorus acid

60. aluminum + phosphoric acid → hydrogen + aluminum phosphate

61. ammonium chloride + sodium nitrite → sodium chloride + nitrogen + water

62. chlorine + sodium hydroxide → sodium chloride + sodium hypochlorite + water

63. lead (II) nitrate (heated) → lead monoxide + nitrogen dioxide + oxygen

64. mercury (I) oxide + oxygen → mercury (II) oxide

65. calcium oxide + magnesium chloride → magnesium oxide + calcium chloride

66. calcium + water → calcium hydroxide + hydrogen

(continued)

67. chromium (III) chloride + sulfuric acid → chromium (III) sulfate + hydrochloric acid

68. iron (III) nitrate + ammonium hydroxide → iron (III) hydroxide + ammonium nitrate

69. aluminum chloride + potassium phosphate → aluminum phosphate + potassium chloride

70. aluminum oxide + carbon + chlorine → carbon monoxide + aluminum chloride

71. copper (I) oxide + hydrochloric acid → copper (I) chloride + water

72. magnesium bicarbonate + hydrochloric acid → magnesium chloride + water + carbon dioxide

73. iron + oxygen → iron (III) oxide

74. silicon + water (heat) → silicon dioxide + hydrogen

75. iron (III) oxide + carbon monoxide → iron + carbon dioxide

76. calcium chloride + chromium (III) nitrate → calcium nitrate + chromium (III) chloride

77. zinc sulfide + oxygen → zinc oxide + sulfur dioxide

78. calcium phosphate + sulfuric acid → calcium sulfate + phosphoric acid

79. iron (III) hydroxide (heated) → iron (III) oxide + water

80. aluminum sulfate + sodium bicarbonate → aluminum hydroxide + sodium sulfate + carbon dioxide

81. calcium phosphate + silicon dioxide + carbon → phosphorus + calcium silicate + carbon monoxide

82. calcium oxide + sulfur dioxide → calcium sulfite

(continued)

83. carbon dioxide + magnesium hydroxide → magnesium carbonate + water

84. calcium oxide + hydrochloric acid → calcium chloride + water

85. calcium carbonate + silicon dioxide → calcium silicate + carbon dioxide

86. antimony + chlorine → antimony trichloride

87. magnesium nitride + water → magnesium hydroxide + ammonia

88. arsenic + oxygen → arsenic (III) oxide

89. ammonium bicarbonate (heated) → ammonia + water + carbon dioxide

90. cupric oxide + ammonia → copper + water + nitrogen

91. ammonium dichromate (heated) → chromium trioxide + nitrogen + water

92. hydrogen sulfide + cadmium nitrate → nitric acid + cadmium sulfide

93. barium bromide + sodium phosphate → barium phosphate + sodium bromide

94. aluminum chloride + ammonium fluoride → aluminum fluoride + ammonium chloride

95. silver nitrate + potassium sulfate → silver sulfate + potassium nitrate

96. bismuth nitrate + calcium iodide → bismuth iodide + calcium nitrate

97. aluminum chromate + ammonium sulfate → ammonium chromate + aluminum sulfate

98. zinc nitrate + ammonium bromide → zinc bromide + ammonium nitrate

99. bismuth nitrate + ammonium hydroxide → bismuth hydroxide + ammonium nitrate

(continued)

100. cadmium nitrate + sulfuric acid → cadmium sulfate + nitric acid

101. zinc + silver iodide → zinc iodide + silver

102. iron (III) chloride + sulfuric acid → iron (III) sulfate + hydrochloric acid

103. bismuth sulfate + ammonium hydroxide → bismuth hydroxide + ammonium sulfate

104. hydrogen iodide + oxygen → iodine + water

105. potassium sulfate + barium chloride → barium sulfate + potassium chloride

106. barium sulfate + carbon → barium sulfide + carbon monoxide

107. aluminum oxide + hydrofluoric acid → aluminum fluoride + water

108. aluminum fluoride + sulfuric acid → aluminum sulfate + hydrogen fluoride

109. potassium iodide + hydrogen peroxide → potassium hydroxide + iodine

110. zinc + ferric sulfate → zinc sulfate + ferrous sulfate

111. lead (II) sulfide + lead monoxide → lead + sulfur dioxide

112. copper + sulfuric acid → copper (II) sulfate + water + sulfur dioxide

113. aluminum hydroxide (heated) → aluminum oxide + water

114. nitrogen + hydrogen → ammonia

115. sodium carbonate + carbonic acid → sodium bicarbonate

116. silicon dioxide + hydrofluoric acid → water + silicon tetrafluoride

(continued)

117. sodium hypochlorite → sodium chloride + sodium chlorate

118. sodium chlorite + chlorine → sodium chloride + chlorine dioxide

119. methane + sulfur dioxide (heated) → hydrogen sulfide + carbon dioxide + hydrogen

120. tellurous acid → tellurium dioxide + water

121. iron (II) selenide + hydrochloric acid → iron (II) chloride + hydrogen selenide

122. magnesium + nitrogen → magnesium nitride

123. silver cyanide + potassium → potassium cyanide + silver

124. copper (II) sulfate + ammonia → cupriammonia sulfate

125. calcium carbide + nitrogen → calcium cyanamide + carbon

126. calcium cyanamide + water → calcium carbonate + ammonia

127. zinc arsenide + hydrochloric acid → arsine + zinc chloride

128. lead (II) hydroxide + sodium stannite → lead + sodium stannate + water

129. sodium silicate + hydrochloric acid → sodium chloride + silicic acid

130. boron trioxide + magnesium → magnesium oxide + boron

131. iron (II) cyanide + potassium cyanide → potassium ferrocyanide

132. sodium aluminate + ammonium chloride → ammonium aluminum oxide + sodium chloride

133. aluminum hydroxide + sodium hydroxide → sodium aluminate + water

(continued)

134. tungsten + chlorine (300° C) → tungsten hexachloride

135. calcium + ammonia → calcium hydride + nitrogen

136. sodium wolframate + sulfuric acid → sodium sulfate + tungstic acid

137. lithium hydride + water → lithium hydroxide + hydrogen

138. boric acid → tetraboric acid + water

139. zinc hydroxide + potassium hydroxide → potassium zincate + water

140. nickel + carbon monoxide → nickel carbonyl

Reaction Prediction

In each of the following examples:

a. State what type of reaction is expected.
b. Tell whether the reaction will occur or not, and why.
c. Write the balanced equation for those reactions that do take place; write the symbols and formulas of the reactants for those reactions that do occur.
d. Indicate whether double replacement reactions are reversible or irreversible.

1. aluminum plus hydrochloric acid
2. calcium hydroxide plus nitric acid
3. aluminum plus magnesium
4. magnesium plus zinc nitrate
5. mercury plus oxygen
6. zinc chloride plus hydrogen sulfide
7. dinitrogen pentoxide plus water
8. silver chloride plus sodium nitrate
9. sodium chlorate (heated)
10. barium nitrate plus sodium chromate
11. sodium bromide plus silver nitrate
12. calcium phosphate plus aluminum sulfate
13. zinc carbonate (heated)

(continued)

14. mercury (I) sulfate plus ammonium nitrate

15. potassium plus fluorine

16. potassium nitrate plus zinc phosphate

17. lithium oxide plus water

18. sodium chloride (electrolyzed)

19. silver plus barium

20. iron (III) hydroxide plus phosphoric acid

21. sodium plus nitric acid

22. iron (III) iodide plus cupric nitrate

23. copper plus sulfuric acid

24. lead plus potassium chlorate

25. sulfur dioxide plus water

26. oxygen plus sulfur

27. sodium sulfate plus barium chloride

28. ammonium phosphate plus lithium hydroxide

29. hydrogen plus oxygen

30. mercury plus nitric acid

(continued)

31. sodium oxide plus water

32. calcium carbonate plus lithium chloride

33. mercury (I) sulfate plus hydrochloric acid

34. potassium nitrate (heated)

35. chlorine plus bromine

36. mercury (I) nitrate plus sodium carbonate

37. magnesium plus hydrochloric acid

38. water (electrolyzed)

39. ammonium nitrite plus barium hydroxide

40. ammonium sulfate plus calcium hydroxide

41. mercury (II) oxide (heated)

42. ammonium phosphate plus aluminum chloride

43. barium oxide plus water

44. iron (III) hydroxide plus nitric acid

45. calcium plus oxygen

46. calcium plus phosphoric acid

(continued)

47. calcium chloride plus ammonium hydroxide

48. aluminum sulfide plus hydrochloric acid

49. magnesium plus sulfur

50. calcium plus aluminum chloride

51. potassium hydroxide plus hydrosulfuric acid

52. sodium carbonate plus sulfuric acid

53. barium sulfate plus calcium chloride

54. silver plus mercurous nitrate

55. barium carbonate (heated)

56. lithium plus bromine

57. sodium chloride plus potassium chromate

58. potassium sulfide plus iron (II) nitrate

59. iodine plus ammonium fluoride

60. sodium plus calcium

61. aluminum chloride (electrolyzed)

62. lead chlorate plus sodium sulfide

63. sulfur trioxide plus water

(continued)

64. calcium carbonate plus hydrochloric acid

65. iron plus sodium bromide

66. ammonium acetate plus iron (II) chloride

67. silver bromide plus ammonium sulfate

68. zinc plus sulfuric acid

69. neon plus potassium

70. iron plus potassium iodide

71. lead (II) hydroxide plus hydrochloric acid

72. iron plus sulfur

73. potassium chlorate (heated)

74. oxygen plus chlorine

75. silver iodide plus iron (III) sulfide

76. ferrous carbonate plus phosphoric acid

77. potassium iodide plus ammonium nitrate

78. potassium plus sodium nitrate (fused)

79. bromine plus sodium chloride

80. silver sulfide plus hydrochloric acid

(continued)

81. magnesium nitrate plus hydrochloric acid

82. ammonia plus hydrogen chloride

83. zinc hydroxide plus sulfuric acid

84. calcium oxide plus water

85. sodium plus chlorine

86. calcium hydroxide (heated)

87. fluorine plus potassium bromide

88. ammonium hydroxide plus sulfuric acid

89. sodium chloride plus potassium nitrate

90. lead plus tin (II) nitrate

91. carbon dioxide plus water

92. chlorine plus lithium bromide

93. lithium hydroxide plus phosphoric acid

94. potassium sulfite plus nitric acid

95. ammonium chloride plus potassium hydroxide

96. strontium carbonate plus nitric acid

97. tin plus mercury (I) nitrate

(continued)

98. ammonium sulfite plus hydrochloric acid

99. magnesium carbonate plus phosphoric acid

100. aluminum sulfite plus hydrochloric acid

Density and Specific Gravity

• *SOLIDS AND LIQUIDS*

1. Copper has a density of 8.9 g/cm^3. What is its specific gravity?

2. 8.0 cm^3 of platinum are found to weigh 171.2 g. Determine the density and specific gravity of platinum.

3. 50.0 cm^3 of lead weigh 565 g. What is the density of lead? The specific gravity?

4. Chloroform has a specific gravity of 1.5. What is its density? What is the weight of 1.0 L of chloroform?

5. 127 mL of turpentine are found to weigh 114.3 g. What is the specific gravity of turpentine?

6. A block of granite of volume 3.8 ft^3 has a weight of 638.30 lb. What is its specific gravity? Its density in the metric system?

7. What is the weight of 137 cm^3 of nickel? The specific gravity of nickel is 8.8.

8. Calculate the specific gravity of marble from the fact that 321 cm^3 of the material weigh 866.7 g.

9. Steel has a specific gravity of 7.8. What volume of steel would weigh 1.00 kg?

10. What is the weight of 2.2 ft^3 of pine wood? The specific gravity of pine wood is 0.4.

11. 78 cm^3 of soft coal weigh 101.4 g. What is its specific gravity?

12. Brass has a specific gravity of 8.5. How much would 10.0 ft^3 of brass weigh?

13. The concentrated sulfuric acid in a 500.0 mL flask weighs 920 g. What is the specific gravity of sulfuric acid?

(continued)

14. 421 cm^3 of water at 4° C are cooled to 0° C. Its new volume is 425 cm^3. What is the density of water at 0° C?

15. Cast iron has a specific gravity of 7.1. What is the density of cast iron in pounds per cubic foot?

16. What is the weight of 62.3 mL of carbon tetrachloride if the specific gravity of carbon tetrachloride is 1.6?

17. Carbon disulfide may be purchased in bottles containing 100.0 lb of the disulfide. These bottles have a volume of 1.27 ft^3. What is the specific gravity of carbon disulfide? What is the weight of 1.00 L of carbon disulfide?

18. 50.0 mL of water at 4° C are frozen to ice. The volume of the ice produced is 46.0 mL. What is the density and specific gravity of the ice?

19. Seawater has a specific gravity of 1.03. A certain sample of seawater was found to weigh 154 g. What was the volume of the water?

20. What is the weight of 5.0 ft^3 of mercury? The specific gravity of mercury is 13.6.

• *GASES AND VAPORS*

NOTE: In the following problems, **air** is the standard used in determining specific gravity.

1. 500.0 mL of hydrogen chloride weigh 0.8196 g. Find the density and specific gravity of this gas.

2. 1.0 L of ammonia weighs 0.7710 g. Find the density and specific gravity of ammonia.

3. The density of nitrous oxide is 1.9778 g/L. Calculate the molecular weight and specific gravity of this gas.

4. The specific gravity of carbon monoxide is 0.967. What is its density and molecular weight?

(continued)

5. The specific gravity of chlorine is 2.49. What is its density and molecular weight?

6. The density of hydrogen is 0.0898 g/L. What is its specific gravity and molecular weight?

7. 250 mL of krypton gas weigh 0.934 g. Find the density, specific gravity, and molecular weight of krypton.

8. Find the weight of 5.0 L of carbon dioxide.

9. The specific gravity of stibine is 4.34. Find the density and molecular weight of this gas.

10. 100.0 mL of silicon tetrafluoride weigh 0.461 g. Find the density, specific gravity, and molecular weight of the gas.

11. Find the density of chlorine.

12. The density of phosphorus trifluoride is 3.90 g/L. Find its specific gravity and molecular weight.

13. Find the weight of 200.0 mL of sulfur monochloride, S_2Cl_2.

14. Determine the specific gravity of methane, CH_4.

15. 400.0 mL of hydrogen iodide weigh 2.28 g. Find the density, specific gravity, and molecular weight.

16. What is the specific gravity of bromine vapor?

17. Find the weight of 100.0 mL of xenon.

18. The specific gravity of carbonyl sulfide, COS, is 2.10. Find its density and molecular weight.

19. The density of an unknown gas is 2.09 g/L. Find its specific gravity and molecular weight.

(continued)

20. 300.0 mL of sulfur dioxide weigh 0.8781 g. Find the density, specific gravity and molecular weight of this gas.

21. The density of helium is 0.1785 g/L. Find the specific gravity and molecular weight of helium.

22. Find the weight of 450.0 mL of hydrogen sulfide.

23. The specific gravity of nitric oxide is 1.037. Find its density and molecular weight.

24. What is the specific gravity of argon?

25. 50.0 mL of oxygen weigh 0.0714 g. Find the density, specific gravity, and molecular weight of oxygen.

26. What is the weight of 285 mL of tellurium hydride, TeH_2?

27. Find the density and specific gravity of nitrogen.

28. The specific gravity of hydrogen fluoride is 0.988. What molecular weight does this give for the compound?

29. What is the weight of 5.2 L of phosgene, $COCl_2$?

30. Calculate the density and specific gravity of hydrogen bromide.

Gas Law Problems

I. Correct the volumes of the dry gases as directed in each of the following problems:

1. Change 125 mL of a gas at 25° C to standard temperature.
2. Change 300.0 mL of a gas at 0.0° C to 30.0° C.
3. Change 220.0 mL of a gas at 10.0° C to 100.0° C.
4. Change 1.00 L of a gas at 32° C to 27° C.
5. Change 100.0 mL of a gas at 740.0 torr pressure to standard pressure.
6. Change 250.0 mL of a gas at standard pressure to 780.0 torr.
7. Change 30.0 mL of a gas at standard pressure to 600.0 torr.
8. Change 750.0 mL of a gas at 700.0 torr to 800.0 torr.
9. Change 500.0 mL of a gas at 60.0° C and 800.0 torr to standard conditions.
10. Change 800.0 mL at 40.0° C and 700.0 mm to standard conditions.
11. Change 60.0 mL at standard conditions to 55° C and 745 torr.
12. Change 35 mL at standard conditions to 25° C and 725 torr.
13. Change 50.0 mL at standard conditions to 43° C and 750 mm.
14. Change 75.0 mL at 100.0° C and 450 torr to standard conditions.
15. Change 10.0 mL at 27° C and 1.25 atm to standard conditions.
16. Change 250 mL at 32° C and 750 torr to 47° C and 780 torr.
17. Change 200.0 mL at 17° C and 800.0 mm to 37° C and 700.0 mm.
18. Change 45 mL at 15° C and 790 torr to 23° C and 810 torr.
19. Change 135 mL at 34° C and 800.0 torr to 20.° C and 760 torr.
20. Change 310 mL at 58° C and 730 torr to 15° C and 750 torr.
21. Change 2.0 L at 43° C and 720 torr to 28° C and 800.0 torr.
22. Change 550 mL at 25° C and 790 mm to 55° C and 700.00 mm.

(continued)

23. Change 20.0 mL at 33° C and 700.0 torr to 57° C and 1.08 atm.

24. Change 150 mL at 0.0° C and 740 torr to 41° C and 750 torr.

25. Change 375 mL at 13° C and 780 torr to 33° C and 760 torr.

26. Change 80.0 mL at 27° C and 150 mm to standard conditions.

27. Change 37.5 mL at –5° C and 600.0 mm to standard conditions.

28. Change 175 mL at 3.0° C and 720 torr to standard conditions.

29. Change 350 mL at –30.° C and 100.0 mm to standard conditions.

30. Change 2.0 L at –45° C and 25 mm to standard conditions.

31. Change 18 mL at standard conditions to 23° C and 740 torr.

32. Change 120. mL at standard conditions to 60.0° C and 85 cm.

33. Change 36 mL at standard conditions to –13° C and 32 cm.

34. Change 3.2 L at standard conditions to 110° C and 720 mm.

35. Change 42 mL at standard conditions to 27° C and 794 torr.

36. Change 272 mL at standard conditions to 31° C and 3.2 atm.

37. Change 4.0 L at standard conditions to –43° C and 420 mm.

38. Change 75 mL at standard conditions to 17° C and 735 torr.

39. Change 360 mL at standard conditions to –19° C and 360 torr.

40. Change 6.5 L at standard conditions to –23° C and 150 mm.

II. What pressure is needed to make the following changes?

1. 130 mL of a dry gas at 740 torr to 150 mL.

2. 25 mL of a dry gas at 65 cm to 30.0 mL.

3. 1.0 L of a dry gas at 70.0 cm to 1.2 L.

4. 75 mL of a dry gas at 4.1 atm and 27° C to 70.0 mL at 25° C.

5. 60.0 mL of a dry gas at 760 torr and 0.0° C to 10.0 mL at 25° C.

6. 400.0 mL of a dry gas at 760 mm and 15° C to 300.0 mL at –30.0° C.

III. What temperature is needed to make the following changes?

1. 30.0 mL of a dry gas at 14° C to 22 mL.
2. 16.4 mL of a dry gas at 28° C to 20.0 mL.
3. 39 mL of a dry gas at 0.0° C to 35 mL.
4. 50.0 mL of a dry gas at 5° C and 760 mm to 55 mL and 780 mm.
5. 1.0 L of a dry gas at 10.0° C and 800.0 torr to 0.50 L and 760 torr.
6. 10.0 mL of a dry gas at 20.0° C and 760 torr to 1.0 mL and 800.0 torr.

IV. Solve the following gas law problems:

1. If 120 mL of oxygen are collected over water at 27° C and 740 mm pressure, what will the volume of the dry gas be at STP?
2. If 500.0 mL of hydrogen are collected over water at 20.0° C and 745 torr, what will the volume of the dry gas be at STP?
3. If 250 mL of nitrogen are collected over water at 25° C and 750 torr, what will the volume of the dry gas be at STP?
4. A certain gas is collected over water at 740 mm and 23° C. The collecting tube is left in place, and the volume is not measured until the next day when the pressure is 745 mm and the temperature 20.0° C, at which time the volume is found to be 15.3 mL. What was the original volume?
5. If 153.48 mL of carbon dioxide are collected over mercury at 14° C and 723 torr, what will its volume be at STP?
6. 113 mL of oxygen are collected over water at 22° C and 741 torr and left in position over night. On the next day, the volume has reduced to 109 mL and the temperature reads 21° C. What is the pressure on the second day?
7. If 18 mL of oxygen are collected over water at 27° C and 740 mm of pressure, what volume will the dry gas have at STP?

(continued)

8. 36 mL of nitrogen are collected over water at 25° C. The barometer is broken and no pressure can be read. Three days later, when a new barometer arrives, the volume of the damp gas has changed to 32 mL at a temperature of 21° C. The barometric reading is 739 torr. What was the original pressure?

V. **Listed below are the densities for a number of gases at standard conditions. Find the new density of the gas in each case at the stated conditions.**

1. carbon dioxide: 1.98 grams per liter (at 40.0° C)

2. helium: 0.178 grams per liter (at 23° C)

3. nitric oxide: 1.34 grams per liter (at 750 mm)

4. hydrogen chloride: 1.64 grams per liter (at 780 torr)

5. acetylene: 1.17 grams per liter (at 37° C and 780 torr)

6. oxygen: 1.43 grams per liter (at 17° C and 740 mm)

7. sulfur dioxide: 2.93 grams per liter (at 25° C and 755 torr)

8. ethylene: 1.26 grams per liter (at 15° C and 70.0 cm)

9. chlorine: 3.21 grams per liter (at 8.0° C and 795 mm)

10. nitrogen: 1.25 grams per liter (at −23° C and 400 torr)

11. ammonia: 0.77 grams per liter (at 500.0° C and 25 cm)

12. methane: 0.717 grams per liter (at 250° C and 4520 torr)

13. hydrogen sulfide: 1.54 grams per liter (at −53° C and 2550 mm)

(continued)

14. hydrogen: 0.09 grams per liter (at 2850° C and 0.010 atm)

15. argon: 1.78 grams per liter (at –150° C and 225 atm)

16. 25 mL of fluorine gas weigh 0.0390 g at 25° C. What is the density of fluorine at standard conditions?

17. Find the density of carbon monoxide gas at standard conditions if $30\bar{0}$ mL of the gas weigh 0.395 g at 800.0 mm of pressure.

18. 10.0 mL of neon would weigh 10.8 g at 10,000.0 torr and –270° C. From this information, calculate the density of neon at standard conditions.

19. The weight of 230 mL of hydrogen at 5.0 atm and –53° C is 0.128 g. What is the density of hydrogen at standard conditions?

20. The weight of 15 mL of nitrous oxide at 50.0 mm and 2000.0° C is 2.3×10^{-4} g. What would 1.0 L of this gas weigh at standard conditions?

21. A student collected a liter flask full of oxygen over water when the thermometer read 23° C and the barometer read 750 mm. Two hours later, the volume of the gas in the flask had reduced to 978 mL although the barometer had not changed. What change had occurred in the temperature?

22. A large balloon containing 400.0 L of hydrogen is released from the earth when the temperature is 21° C and the pressure 760 mm. What volume will the gas occupy when it reaches the atmospheric level at which the temperature is –67° C and the pressure 125 torr.

23. Suppose the balloon in problem 22 reached the given level, but the temperature was +67° C instead of –67° C. (All other conditions as stated in 22.) What volume would the hydrogen occupy then?

24. A quantity of nitrogen gas is enclosed in a tightly stoppered 500.0 mL flask at room temperature (20.0° C) and 760 mm pressure. The flask is then heated to 680° C. If the flask can withstand pressures of less than 3 atm, will it explode under this heating?

(continued)

25. A 1.0 L rubber bladder is filled with carbon dioxide gas in a warm (25° C) room (pressure = 745 torr). What volume will the gas occupy when it is taken out into the open air where the temperature is −12° C and the pressure, 742 torr?

26. 500.0 mL of air are trapped in a tube over mercury at 25° C. It is found that, after six days, the air has expanded so that 32 mL have escaped from the tube. What total temperature change occurred over this period if the pressure remained constant?

27. A rubber balloon containing 1.0 L of gas is carried from the top of a mountain to the bottom of the mountain, where its volume is measured as 0.85 L at standard pressure. Assuming that there was no temperature change during the trip, what was the pressure at the top of the mountain?

28. A sudden cold snap in June causes Mr. Van Dellen to order a 15 L tank of butane gas for his cottage heater. The temperature on this day was 18° C and the atmospheric pressure, 743 mm. Assuming that some type of piston arrangement was built into the tank so that the gas could expand freely, what volume would the butane gas occupy a week later when the temperature reached 42° C and 721 mm of pressure (assume 3.0 L of gas had been used)?

29. A toy balloon containing 425 mL of air escapes from a little boy watching a parade. The temperature is 32° C at street level and the pressure is 745 torr. When the balloon stops rising, its volume has become 895 mL although the atmospheric pressure has decreased by only 300.0 torr. What is the temperature at this level?

30. To what temperature must 15 L of oxygen gas at 0.0° C be heated at 1.00 atm pressure in order to occupy a volume of 23 L, assuming that the pressure increases by 5.0 mm?

VI. Solve the following problems involving the ideal gas law equation.

1. What pressure is exerted by 1.0 mol of an ideal gas contained in a 1.0 L vessel at 0.0° C?

2. What volume will 5.0 mol of an ideal gas occupy at 25.0° C and 1.5 atm of pressure?

3. Calculate the molecular weight of a gas if 4.5 L of the gas at 785 torr and 23.5° C weigh 13.5 g.

(continued)

4. 0.453 mol of a gas confined to a 15.0 L container exerts a pressure of 1.24 atm on the walls of the container. What is the temperature of the gas?

5. 5.4 g of carbon dioxide gas are confined to a 20.0 L container at a temperature of 32.5° C. What pressure does the gas exert?

6. 2.125 g of a gas in a 1.25 L container exert a pressure of 0.838 atm at 40.0° C. What is the molecular weight of the gas?

7. To what temperature must 10.0 g of ammonia gas have to be heated in a 15.0 L container in order for it to exert a pressure of 3.50 atm?

8. 2.0×10^{-5} g of hydrogen gas at 155° C exert a pressure of 322.5 torr on the walls of a small cylindrical tube. What is the volume of the tube?

VII. Listed below are various combinations of (1) molar composition of a gas mixture (m_A, m_B, m_C, etc.), (2) partial pressure of each gas in the mixture (p_A, p_B, p_C, etc.), and (3) the total pressure of the mixture (p_T). From this information, calculate any of the variables which are not given.

1. p_T = 785 mm; m_A = 45%; m_B = 55%

2. p_T = 1.050 atm; m_A = 38%; m_B = 40%; m_C = 22%

3. p_A = 420 torr; p_B = 180 torr; p_C = 200 torr

4. p_T = 1.12 atm; p_A = 0.43 atm (two gases only)

5. m_A = 21%; m_B = 34%; m_C = 45%; p_A = 183 torr

6. 10.0 g of carbon dioxide; 15.0 g of nitrogen; p_T = 1.142 atm

7. 5.0 g of argon; 5.0 g of xenon; 5.0 g of krypton; p_{Ar} = 86.4 torr

8. p_T = 1.28 atm; 3.4×10^{-3} g sulfur dioxide; 1.8×10^{-3} g carbon dioxide; 4.0×10^{-2} g nitrogen

VIII. Find the relative rate of diffusion between each of the following pairs of gases.

1. hydrogen and nitrogen
2. oxygen and carbon dioxide
3. hydrogen and carbon dioxide
4. nitrogen and oxygen
5. hydrogen chloride and chlorine
6. carbon monoxide and carbon dioxide

IX. Listed below are (1) the relative rate of diffusion between two gases and (2) the density of the less dense gas. From this information, calculate the density of the more dense gas.

1. 1.14; 1.93 g/L
2. 2.04; 1.28 g/L
3. 1.42; 1.13 g/L
4. 1.85; 1.62 g/L
5. 1.63; 1.46 g/L
6. 1.55; 1.39 g/L

Molecular Weight and Mole Calculations

I. Find the molecular weight or formula weight for each of the compounds shown below:

1. H_3PO_4
2. $AlCl_3$
3. $Dy(OH)_3$
4. $K_2C_4H_4O_6$
5. H_2SO_4
6. N_2O_5
7. $CuSO_4 \cdot 5H_2O$
8. $NiSO_4$
9. $Sn(OH)_4$
10. $(NH_4)_3PO_4$
11. $Fe(C_2H_3O_2)_3$
12. SO_2
13. $KAl(SO_4)_2 \cdot 12H_2O$
14. $NaIO_4$
15. $Pr(OH)_3$
16. $K_4Fe(CN)_6$
17. Nd_2O_3
18. $Sb(NO_3)_3$
19. K_3PO_4
20. $Ga_2(SO_4)_3$
21. zinc acetate
22. copper (I) sulfate
23. carbon dioxide
24. calcium bicarbonate
25. nitric acid
26. aluminum nitrate
27. ammonium sulfate
28. barium chloride dihydrate
29. ferrous phosphate
30. strontium hydroxide
31. sodium sulfite
32. magnesium nitride

(continued)

33. hydrochloric acid

34. ferric sulfate

35. lead (II) bromide

36. cesium chloride

37. copper (II) nitrate

38. magnesium bromide

39. iron (III) hydroxide

40. ammonium carbonate

II. Express each of the following in grams.

1. 1.0 mol of KBr

2. 1.0 mol of $CaCl_2$

3. 2.0 mol of AlF_3

4. 0.50 mol of KNO_3

5. 0.30 mol of $NaHCO_3$

6. 0.25 mol of potassium iodate

7. 0.10 mol of iron (III) carbonate

8. 0.20 mol of sodium sulfate decahydrate

9. 8.0 mol of sodium dihydrogen phosphate

10. 0.30 mol of phosphorus pentachloride

11. 1.50 mol of HCl

12. 0.736 mol of H_2SO_4

13. 0.042 mol of KOH

14. 0.147 mol of NH_4OH

15. 1.26×10^{-4} mol of $HC_2H_3O_2$

(continued)

16. 2.6 mol of lithium bromide

17. 0.395 mol of magnesium nitrate

18. 2.4×10^{-3} mol of sodium phosphate

19. 4.6×10^{-3} mol of ammonium chloride

20. 3.85×10^{-6} mol of lead (II) ions

III. Convert each of the following to its equivalent in moles.

1. 86.84 g of LiBr

2. 62.3 g of MgF_2

3. 17.1 g of H_2S

4. 302.7 g of $ScCl_3$

5. 8.5 g of PH_3

6. 33.4 g of KNO_3

7. 17.2 g of H_3PO_4

8. 38.1 g of $FeCl_3$

9. 15.9 g of $Ca(NO_3)_2$

10. 8.8 g of potassium carbonate

11. 5.0 g of ammonium sulfate

12. 2.5 g of copper (II) chloride

13. 30.0 g of tin (II) nitrate

14. 0.257 g of arsenic pentachloride

(continued)

15. 48.8 g of lanthanum nitrate

16. 0.2000 g of cadmium bromide

17. 1.50 x 10^{-4} g of lanthanum nitrate

18. 0.0350 g of potassium permanganate

19. 10.00 g of ammonium dichromate

20. 8.045 g of titanium tetrachloride

Percentage Composition

Find the percentage composition of each of the following compounds:

1. $NaCl$
2. HBr
3. KI
4. CO
5. SO_2
6. H_2Te
7. K_2S
8. AlI_3
9. NH_3
10. NH_4Br
11. $NaNO_3$
12. H_2SO_4
13. $Ca(NO_3)_2$
14. $Sc(OH)_3$
15. K_3PO_4
16. $Zn_3(PO_4)_2$
17. Fe_3O_4
18. $(NH_4)_2SO_4$
19. $CuSO_4 \cdot 5H_2O$
20. $(NH_4)_2Cr_2O_7$
21. potassium bromide
22. cesium chloride
23. nitric oxide
24. hydriodic acid
25. carbon dioxide
26. water
27. sodium oxide
28. phosphorus tribromide
29. arsine
30. potassium nitrite
31. ammonium chloride
32. phosphoric acid
33. barium hydroxide
34. aluminum nitrate

(continued)

35. lithium phosphate

36. calcium phosphate

37. aluminum oxide

38. ammonium carbonate

39. ammonium phosphate

40. barium chloride dihydrate

41. What is the percentage of strontium in $SrCl_2$?

42. What is the percentage of carbon in calcium carbonate?

43. What is the percentage of water in cupric sulfate pentahydrate?

44. What is the percentage of hydrogen in $Ca(C_2H_3O_2)_2$?

45. What is the percentage of oxygen in $KMnO_4$?

46. What is the percentage of cobalt in cobaltous nitrate?

47. What is the percentage of carbon in sucrose, $C_{12}H_{22}O_{11}$?

48. What is the percentage of bismuth in sodium bismuthate, $NaBiO_3$?

49. What is the percentage of aluminum in $NaAl(SO_4)_2 \cdot 12H_2O$?

50. What is the percentage of chromium in potassium dichromate?

51. How much iron can be obtained from 100.0 g of Fe_3O_4?

52. How much phosphorus is there in 500.0 g of calcium phosphate?

53. How many pounds of aluminum can be obtained from 1.00 ton of aluminum chloride?

54. How many grams of hydrogen can be obtained from 35 mL of water?

55. How much anhydrous cupric sulfate can be obtained from 15.0 g of hydrated cupric sulfate?

56. How many pounds of silver can be recovered from 10.0 pounds of silver sulfide?

57. How much lead can be extracted from 200.0 lb of its ore, lead sulfide?

(continued)

58. Free hydrogen gas can be obtained from ethyl alcohol, C_2H_5OH. How many grams of hydrogen would be obtained from 150.0 g of the alcohol?

59. How many grams of water are driven off by the heating of 125 g of cobaltous chloride hexahydrate?

60. Can 18 g of oxygen be obtained by heating 50.0 g of potassium chlorate?

Empirical Formula

Find the empirical formula for each of the following substances. The percentage composition is given.

1. 88.8% copper; 11.2% oxygen
2. 40.0% carbon; 6.7% hydrogen; 53.3% oxygen
3. 92.3% carbon; 7.7% hydrogen
4. 70.0% iron; 30.0% oxygen
5. 5.88% hydrogen; 94.12% oxygen
6. 79.90% copper; 20.10% oxygen
7. 56.4% potassium; 8.7% carbon; 34.9% oxygen
8. 10.04% carbon; 0.84% hydrogen; 89.12% chlorine
9. 42.50% chromium; 57.50% chlorine
10. 15.8% carbon; 84.2% sulfur
11. 30.43% nitrogen; 69.57% oxygen
12. 82.40% nitrogen; 17.60% hydrogen
13. 12.5% hydrogen; 37.5% carbon; 50.0% oxygen
14. 75.0% carbon; 25.0% hydrogen
15. 29.40% calcium; 23.56% sulfur; 47.04% oxygen
16. 38.67% potassium; 13.85% nitrogen; 47.48% oxygen
17. 60.0% magnesium; 40.0% oxygen

(continued)

18. 52.94% aluminum; 47.06% oxygen

19. 72.40% iron; 27.60% oxygen

20. 52.0% zinc; 9.6% carbon; 38.4% oxygen

21. 60.98% arsenic; 39.02% sulfur

22. 74.17% mercury; 25.83% chlorine

23. 60.0% terbium; 40.0% chlorine

24. 65.1% scandium; 34.9% oxygen

25. 34.6% gallium; 17.8% carbon; 47.6% oxygen

26. A sample of potassium sulfate has the following composition: 17.96 g of potassium, 7.35 g of sulfur, 14.70 g of oxygen. What is its simplest formula?

27. A pure sample of mercury oxide produced 20.3 g of mercury and 1.7 g of oxygen. What oxide of mercury is this?

28. 11.00 g of a certain compound contain 2.82 g of magnesium and 8.18 g of chlorine. What is its simplest formula?

29. A certain sample of a barium salt contains 8.57 g of barium and 4.43 g of chlorine. What is its simplest formula?

30. 50.0 g of sulfur are mixed with 100.0 g of iron and the mixture is heated. When the reaction is completed, 12.7 g of iron remain. What is the formula of the compound formed?

31. 0.916 g of iron is heated in air. The resulting product weighs 1.178 g. What is the formula of the compound?

32. 21.42 g of calcium combine with 8.58 g of oxygen in a combustion reaction. What is the formula of the product?

33. 0.238 g of carbon is burned in 1.00 L of oxygen. The oxide of carbon which is formed weighs 0.872 g. What is the formula of this oxide?

34. Analysis of 100.0 g of a compound produces the following result: 26.6 g of potassium; 35.4 g of chromium; 38.0 g of oxygen. What is the formula of this compound?

35. When 0.982 g of mercuric oxide are heated until all oxygen is expelled, 0.909 g of mercury remain. What is the formula of this oxide?

Molecular Formula

I. Given below are the percentage compositions for a number of compounds. From this information determine the simplest formula for each compound. Use the density information to determine the correct formulas for these compounds.

1. 27.3% carbon; 72.7% oxygen; 1.0 L weighs 1.96 g
2. 92.3% carbon; 7.7% hydrogen; 500.0 mL weigh 1.72 g
3. 94.12% sulfur; 5.88% hydrogen; vapor density = 17.0
4. 47.4% sulfur; 52.6% chlorine; 50.0 mL weigh 0.301 g
5. 30.43% nitrogen; 69.57% oxygen; 250 mL weigh 1.035 g
6. 95% fluorine; 5% hydrogen; 100.0 mL weigh 0.18 g
7. 46.6% nitrogen; 53.4% oxygen; 300.0 mL weigh 0.40 g
8. 85.72% carbon; 14.28% hydrogen; 2.0 L weigh 2.50 g
9. 37.6% carbon; 12.5% hydrogen; 49.9% oxygen; 60.0 mL weigh 0.86 g
10. 10.04% carbon; 0.84% hydrogen; 89.12% chlorine; 1.0 L weighs 5.30 g
11. 46.2% carbon; 53.8% nitrogen; 219 mL weigh 0.508 g
12. 42.9% carbon; 57.1% oxygen; 400.0 mL weigh 0.50 g
13. 40.00% carbon; 6.67% hydrogen; 53.33% oxygen; 10.0 mL weigh 0.027 g
14. 80.0% carbon; 20.0% hydrogen; 150 mL weigh 0.20 g
15. 73.8% carbon; 8.7% hydrogen; 17.5% nitrogen; 100.0 mL weigh 0.72 g

II. Given below are the percentage compositions for a number of compounds. From this information, determine the simplest formula for each compound. Use the freezing and boiling point information to determine the correct formulas for these compounds. All of the compounds are non-ionizable organic compounds.

1. benzylamine: 78.5% carbon; 13.1% nitrogen; 8.4% hydrogen; 107 g dissolved in 1000 g of water have a freezing point of −1.86° C.

2. 2,3-butadione: 55.8% carbon; 7.0% hydrogen; 37.2% oxygen; 86 g dissolved in 1000 g of water have a boiling point of 100.52° C.

3. t-butyl alcohol: 64.9% carbon; 13.5% hydrogen; 21.7% oxygen; 37 g dissolved in 500 g of water have a freezing point of −1.86° C.

4. ethyl caprate: 72.0% carbon; 12.0% hydrogen; 16% oxygen; the boiling point of 50 g of this compound in 250 g of water is 100.52° C.

5. urotropin: 51.4% carbon; 8.6% hydrogen; 40.0% nitrogen; 14 g dissolved in 100 g of water have a boiling point of 100.52° C.

6. isocrotonic acid: 55.8% carbon; 7.0% hydrogen; 37.2% oxygen; 25.8 g in 300 g of water have a freezing point of −1.86° C.

7. isosuccinic acid: 40.6% carbon; 5.1% hydrogen; 54.3% oxygen; 29.5 g dissolved in 500 g of water have a freezing point of −0.93° C.

8. ketine: 67.6% carbon; 7.4% hydrogen; 25.9% nitrogen; 10.8 g dissolved in 400 g of water have a boiling point of 100.13° C.

9. alpha naphthalenedisulfonic acid: 41.7% carbon; 2.8% hydrogen; 22.2% sulfur; 33.3% oxygen; the freezing point of 43.2 g of this compound dissolved in 600 g of water is −0.465° C.

10. nicotine: 74.0% carbon; 8.6% hydrogen; 17.3% nitrogen; 12.2 g dissolved in 250 g of water have a freezing point of −0.56° C.

11. nitralinic acid: 31.3% carbon; 0.9% hydrogen; 55.7% oxygen; 12.2% nitrogen; 11.5 g of this compound dissolved in 150 g of water have a boiling point of 100.17° C.

12. oxalic acid: 26.7% carbon; 2.2% hydrogen; 71.1% oxygen; the freezing point of a solution of 51.3 g of oxalic acid in 200 g of water is −5.30° C.

(continued)

13. piperazinium salt of oxalic acid: 41.0% carbon; 6.8% hydrogen; 15.9% nitrogen; 36.4% oxygen; 250 g of this compound dissolved in 300 g of water have a boiling point of 102.45° C.

14. paraldol: 54.6% carbon; 9.0% hydrogen; 36.4% oxygen; 358 g of this compound dissolved in 400 g of water have a freezing point of −9.50° C.

15. diacetone alcohol: 62.1% carbon; 10.4% hydrogen; 27.5% oxygen; 56.1 g dissolved in 150 g of water have a freezing point of −6.0° C.

Stoichiometry

***In problems involving reduction with* carbon, *assume the* carbon *is completely oxidized to* carbon dioxide.**

• *WEIGHT-WEIGHT PROBLEMS*

1. Carbon dioxide is produced in the reaction between calcium carbonate and hydrochloric acid. How many grams of calcium carbonate would be needed to react completely with 15.0 grams of hydrochloric acid? How many grams of carbon dioxide would be produced in this reaction? How many grams of calcium chloride would be formed at the same time?

2. Sulfur dioxide may be catalytically oxidized to sulfur trioxide. How many grams of sulfur dioxide could be converted by this process if 100.0 g of oxygen are available for the oxidation?

3. Lightning discharges in the atmosphere catalyze the conversion of nitrogen to nitric oxide. How many grams of nitrogen would be required to make 25.0 g of nitric oxide in this way?

4. Ferric oxide may be reduced to pure iron either with carbon monoxide or with coke (pure carbon). Suppose that 150.0 lb of ferric oxide are available. How many pounds of carbon monoxide would be required to reduce the oxide? How many pounds of coke would be needed? In each case, how many pounds of pure iron would be produced?

5. Zinc metal will react with either hydrochloric or sulfuric acid to produce hydrogen gas. If 50.0 g of zinc are to be used in the reaction, how much of each acid would be needed to completely react with all of the zinc? How much hydrogen gas (in grams) would be produced in each case?

6. Calcium phosphate, silicon dioxide, and coke may be heated together in an electric furnace to produce phosphorus, as shown in the following equation:

$$2\ Ca_3(PO_4)_2 + 6\ SiO_2 + 10C \rightarrow 6\ CaSiO_3 + 10\ CO\uparrow + P_4$$

(continued)

In this reaction, how many pounds of calcium phosphate would be needed to make 100.0 lb of phosphorus? How much calcium silicate would be formed as a by-product? How much sand would be used up in this same reaction?

7. Phosphoric acid is produced in the reaction between calcium phosphate and sulfuric acid. How much of the phosphoric acid would be produced from 55 g of the calcium phosphate? What other product is formed and in what quantity?

8. Phosphine, PH_3, is formed when calcium phosphide is added to water. How many grams of phosphine can be obtained from 200.0 g of calcium phosphide? How many grams of the other product are formed?

9. Coke will reduce hot arsenious oxide to pure arsenic (As_4). How much coke would be required to completely reduce 500.0 lb of the oxide? How much arsenic is recovered from this reaction?

10. How much iron will be required to release all of the antimony from 10.0 g antimony trisulfide? How much antimony is obtained in this reaction? (Ferrous sulfide is formed)

11. Sodium tetraborate is produced according to the following reaction:

$$4\ H_3BO_3 + 2\ NaOH \rightarrow 7\ H_2O + Na_2B_4O_7$$

How much boric acid is needed to make 150 tons of sodium tetraborate?

12. Calcium oxide can be prepared by heating calcium in oxygen. How much calcium would be needed to make 15.0 g of calcium oxide in this way?

13. If the calcium oxide were prepared by heating calcium carbonate, how much of the carbonate would be required to produce the 15.0 g of the oxide?

(continued)

14. If the calcium oxide were to be obtained by the heating of calcium hydroxide, how much hydroxide would be needed to obtain the 15.0 g?

15. If the 15.0 g of calcium oxide in the above problems were allowed to react with water, what amount of calcium hydroxide would be produced?

16. How much magnesium sulfate is needed to completely react with 145 g of sodium chloride? How much sodium sulfate could be produced by this reaction?

17. In nature, carbon dioxide in the atmosphere reacts with calcium hydroxide to produce calcium carbonate. This calcium carbonate will react with carbonic acid (carbon dioxide and water) to form calcium bicarbonate. What weight of calcium bicarbonate would eventually be produced by the action of carbon dioxide on 1.0 g of calcium hydroxide?

18. Hard water, containing calcium bicarbonate as hardness, may be softened by adding sodium hydroxide. Sodium carbonate, calcium carbonate, and water all are formed in the reaction. What weight of sodium hydroxide would be needed to react with all the calcium bicarbonate formed in problem 17?

19. Permanent hard water contains calcium sulfate and can be softened by the addition of sodium carbonate. What amount of sodium carbonate would have to be added to react with 1.0 lb of calcium sulfate?

20. Beryllium hydroxide is amphoteric. It reacts with hydrochloric acid to give beryllium chloride and with sodium hydroxide to give sodium beryllate (Na_2BeO_2). If 20.0 grams of beryllium hydroxide are available, how many grams of beryllium chloride can be prepared? How many grams of sodium beryllate could be made? How many grams of hydrochloric acid and sodium hydroxide would be required for these reactions, respectively?

21. The rare earth element terbium may be prepared by the electrolysis of its fused chloride (valence of terbium = 3). How many grams of the chloride would be needed to supply 1.00 g of the pure metal?

(continued)

22. Gadolinium, europium, and samarium may all be prepared in the same way as terbium. How much of the chloride would be required, in each case, to produce 10.0 μg of the pure element? All of these elements have a valence of 3.

23. The metals manganese, chromium, indium, and tin are all prepared by the reduction of their oxides with carbon. How much carbon will be needed to reduce 100.0 lb of each of the following oxides: manganese dioxide, chromic oxide, indium oxide, stannous oxide, stannic oxide?

24. Lanthanum and cerium may be obtained in the free state by fusing their respective chlorides with metallic potassium. What amount of the chloride is needed in each case if it is desired to make 1.0 kg of the metal?

25. How much anhydrous copper (II) sulfate may be obtained by heating 100.0 g of hydrated cupric sulfate?

26. How much mercury metal can be obtained in the reaction between tin (II) chloride and mercury (II) chloride? How much tin (IV) chloride is obtained in the same reaction? Assume that excess tin (II) chloride was permitted to react with 5.0 g of mercuric chloride.

27. Gold will dissolve in the acid mixture known as aqua regia according to the following reaction:

$$Au + HNO_3 + 3\ HCl \rightarrow AuCl_3 + NO\uparrow + 2\ H_2O$$

How much auric chloride will be produced in this reaction when one starts with 5.0 mg of gold? How much nitric acid must be added initially to dissolve all this gold?

28. How many tons of coke (carbon) are needed to reduce 100.0 tons of lead monoxide to free lead?

29. How much silver bromide can be precipitated by the action of 15.0 g of silver nitrate on an excess of sodium bromide?

(continued)

30. How many grams of sulfuric acid will react exactly with 400.0 g of aluminum metal?

31. 100.0 g of a 50-50 mixture of sodium chloride and potassium nitrate are allowed to react. Which reactant is in excess and by how much?

32. 75 g of potassium hydroxide are permitted to react with 50.0 g of hydrochloric acid. How much potassium chloride is formed?

33. 120.0 g of sulfuric acid are added to 230.0 g of barium peroxide. Which reactant is in excess and by how much? How much barium sulfate is precipitated in this reaction?

34. 10.0 g of hydrogen and 75 g of oxygen are exploded together in a reaction tube. How much water is produced? What other gas is found in the tube (besides water vapor) after the reaction, and how much of this gas is there?

35. 50.0 g of oxygen are available for the combustion of 25 g of carbon. Is this an adequate amount? If so, by how much in excess is the oxygen? If not, by how much is the carbon in excess?

36. 75.0 g of zinc are added to 120 g of sulfuric acid. How much hydrogen gas is evolved?

37. 100.0 g of lithium metal are dropped into 1.00 L of water. How much hydrogen is produced?

38. How much ammonia is evolved when 34 g of ammonium chloride are added to 37 g of potassium hydroxide?

39. How many grams of carbon dioxide can be obtained from the action of 100.0 g of sulfuric acid on 100.0 g of calcium carbonate?

(continued)

40. Are 15 g of chlorine gas enough to replace 30.0 g of bromine from a solution of sodium bromide?

41. Will 100.0 g of copper completely replace all the silver in 200.0 g of silver nitrate?

42. Will 45 g of calcium chloride completely precipitate silver chloride from 100.0 g of silver nitrate?

• *WEIGHT-VOLUME PROBLEMS*

1. Hydrogen sulfide may be prepared in the laboratory by the action of hydrochloric acid on iron (II) sulfide. How much iron (II) sulfide would be needed to prepare 15 L of hydrogen sulfide?

2. When hydrogen sulfide is burned, two different reactions may occur:

$$2\ H_2S + O_2 \rightarrow 2\ H_2O + 2\ S \qquad \text{or} \qquad 2\ H_2S + 3\ O_2 \rightarrow 2\ H_2O + 2\ SO_2 \uparrow$$

Assuming that 100.0 g of oxygen were available for this reaction, how much hydrogen sulfide (in liters) could be oxidized in each case? How many grams of sulfur would be produced in the first reaction? How many liters of sulfur dioxide would be produced in the second reaction?

3. When magnesium burns in air, it reacts with both the oxygen and the nitrogen in the air, forming magnesium oxide and magnesium nitride. If 20.0 L of air are used in this reaction, what weight of magnesium oxide is formed? What weight of the nitride is produced?

4. How many liters of nitrogen gas can be produced by the decomposition of 50.0 g ammonium nitrite? Water is the second product.

5. 250 L of hydrogen are used to reduce copper (II) oxide. What weight of copper is to be expected?

(continued)

6. The Haber and Claude processes are methods by which ammonia is synthesized from its elements. What weight of ammonia (in kilograms) is to be expected when 4000.0 L of nitrogen are used in these processes?

7. When ammonia is oxidized in the Ostwald process, nitric acid and water are produced. What weight of nitric acid will be formed when 1500.0 L of ammonia are used?

8. How many liters of oxygen gas can be obtained from the thermal decomposition of 500.0 g of potassium chlorate?

9. What volume of oxygen can be obtained by the addition of excess water to 1.0 g of sodium peroxide?

10. What is the total volume of water gas produced when excess steam is passed over 50.0 g of hot carbon?

11. How much lithium must be added to water in order to obtain 15 L of hydrogen?

12. How much hydrochloric acid must be added to an excess of zinc arsenide in order to obtain 10.0 L of arsine (AsH_3)?

13. How many grams of arsenic can be obtained from the decomposition of 12 L of arsine?

14. It is desired to prepare 100.0 g of silicon tetrafluoride by adding hydrogen fluoride to silicon dioxide. How many liters of hydrogen fluoride will be required for this process?

15. Pure boron can be obtained by the reduction of boron trichloride with hydrogen. How much hydrogen (in liters) is necessary for this process if 500.0 g of boron trichloride are available for the process?

(continued)

16. When black gunpowder explodes, potassium nitrate, carbon, and sulfur react with each other to form nitrogen, carbon dioxide, and potassium sulfide. If the original mixture contains 50.0 g of potassium nitrate, what is the total volume of the gases produced in the reaction?

17. How many liters of hydrogen gas are required to convert 5 g of stannic chloride to stannous chloride? The second product is hydrogen chloride.

18. When ammonia is passed over hot calcium, calcium hydride (CaH_2), and free nitrogen gas are formed. If 30.0 L of nitrogen can be recovered from this reaction, what weight of calcium was originally used?

19. Calcium nitride will react with water to form ammonia and calcium hydroxide. How many grams of the nitride must be used initially in order to prepare 100.0 L of ammonia?

20. Very hot zinc will react with steam to form zinc oxide and hydrogen. What volume of steam would be necessary in order to use up 20.0 g of zinc completely? What volume of hydrogen would be produced in this case?

• *VOLUME-VOLUME PROBLEMS*

1. How many liters of hydrogen gas are needed to react completely with 50 L of chlorine gas? How many liters of hydrogen chloride are produced in this reaction?

2. What volume of oxygen is needed to completely oxidize 25 L of carbon monoxide? How much carbon dioxide is produced?

3. 200 L of ammonia are produced in the reaction between nitrogen and hydrogen. How many liters of each of these gases were used up in this reaction?

(continued)

4. 5 L of nitrogen and 15 L of oxygen are introduced into a reaction tube and then ignited. What volume of nitric oxide is produced? Which of the two original gases is entirely used up? How much of the other gas remains?

5. Will 30.0 L of fluorine gas completely react with 50.0 L of hydrogen gas? Which gas is in excess and by how much? How much hydrogen fluoride (in liters) is formed in this reaction?

6. In the preparation of sulfuric acid, sulfur dioxide must be catalytically oxidized to sulfur trioxide. How much oxygen must be available to convert 50.0 L of sulfur dioxide according to this process?

7. Nitric oxide converts spontaneously to nitrogen dioxide by combining with atmospheric oxygen. If nitric oxide escapes from a bottle at the rate of 7 L/min, at what rate is nitrogen dioxide being produced?

8. It is found in the preparation of water gas from steam and hot carbon that carbon monoxide is being formed at the rate of 30 L/s. At what rate, then, is the hydrogen being produced in the same reaction?

• *COMBINATIONS*

1. Vanadium metal is prepared by reducing vanadium chloride (VCl_2) with hydrogen. How many liters of hydrogen are needed to release 1.0 g of vanadium metal? How many grams of vanadium chloride are needed for this operation?

2. The Solvay process is an important commercial method of preparing sodium carbonate. In the first step of this process, ammonia, water, and carbon dioxide react to produce ammonium bicarbonate. This product is then treated in the second step with sodium chloride to allow conversion to sodium bicarbonate. Finally, the sodium bicarbonate is heated, and sodium carbonate, carbon dioxide, and water are produced. If this process is initiated with a stream of ammonia flowing at the rate of 40.0 L/s, at what rate must carbon dioxide be supplied in the first step? How much sodium chloride (in grams per second) is required to permit

(continued)

the second step to occur as required? Finally, how much sodium carbonate (in grams) and how much carbon dioxide (in liters) are formed every second under these conditions?

3. 200.0 g of sodium chloride are fused and electrolyzed. How many grams of sodium and how many liters of chlorine are obtained in this process?

4. How many grams of magnesium metal are needed to react completely with 50.0 g of phosphoric acid? How many liters of hydrogen are produced?

5. It is desired to prepare 50.0 g of water by synthesis. How many liters of hydrogen must be used? How many liters of oxygen?

6. An unknown amount of potassium chlorate was heated until no more oxygen was evolved. 15.824 g of potassium chloride remained in the test tube. What weight of potassium chlorate had originally been placed in the tube? What volume of oxygen gas was evolved during the experiment?

7. How many grams of carbon can be completely burned in 15 L of oxygen? How many liters of carbon dioxide gas are produced in this reaction?

8. What volume of chlorine gas is needed to completely replace 45 g of bromine from sodium bromide? How many grams of sodium chloride are produced simultaneously?

9. Concentrated hydrochloric acid reacts with manganese dioxide to produce chlorine, manganous chloride ($MnCl_2$), and water. How many grams of manganese dioxide are needed in this reaction if it is desired to collect 20.0 L of chlorine gas? What weight of manganous chloride will be formed?

10. How many grams of magnesium metal are required to liberate 250 mL of hydrogen gas from hydrochloric acid? Exactly how much acid would be used up in this reaction?

(continued)

11. 45 g of mercury (II) oxide are heated until no more oxygen is produced. What volume of oxygen is expected in this case? How much mercury would you expect to collect at the same time?

12. When ammonia reacts with hydrogen chloride (gas), a white solid, ammonium chloride, is formed. How much ammonium chloride would be produced when 500.0 mL of ammonia are used? What volume of hydrogen chloride is needed to carry out this reaction?

Ionic Equations

I. **Write five ionic equations to show the process of ionization.**

II. **Write five ionic equations which show the process of dissociation.**

III. **Write either an ionic or a molecular formula, whichever is correct, for each of the following compounds:**

1. hydrogen sulfide
2. glycerol
3. lithium chloride
4. potassium hydroxide
5. hydrogen cyanide
6. potassium phosphate
7. beryllium hydroxide
8. calcium iodide
9. hydrogen chloride
10. potassium sulfite
11. ammonium bromide
12. carbon tetrachloride
13. calcium hydroxide
14. strontium bromide
15. sodium fluoride
16. hydrogen iodide
17. sodium dihydrogen phosphate
18. sodium sulphate
19. boric acid
20. sucrose
21. samarium bromide
22. hydrogen selenide

(continued)

23. potassium bromide

24. methane

25. ammonium chloride

IV. **Write ionic equations (where they can be used) to show what happens when each of the following substances is put into water:**

1. sodium chloride
2. barium hydroxide
3. calcium chloride
4. hydrogen iodide
5. ammonium bromide
6. potassium carbonate
7. sodium hydroxide
8. benzoic acid ($HC_7H_5O_2$)
9. methyl alcohol (CH_3OH)
10. sodium phosphate
11. hydrogen telluride
12. potassium iodide
13. strontium hydroxide
14. ethyl alcohol (C_2H_5OH)
15. hydrogen bromide
16. glycol ($C_2H_4(OH)_2$)
17. ferrous iodide
18. sulfuric acid
19. magnesium fluoride
20. aluminum chloride
21. disodium hydrogen phosphate
22. acetic acid
23. ammonium sulfate
24. lithium fluoride
25. formic acid ($HCHO_2$)

V. **Write ionic and net ionic equations for each of the following reactions.**

1. potassium chloride + sodium nitrate

2. rubidium hydroxide + hydrochloric acid

3. lithium chlorate + ammonium chloride

4. calcium chloride + sodium carbonate

5. calcium carbonate + cesium chloride

6. ammonium carbonate + hydriodic acid

7. aluminum bromide + cadmium nitrate

8. copper (II) iodide + ammonium sulfate

9. iron (III) sulfate + lead (II) chlorate

10. sodium hydroxide + sulfuric acid

11. strontium chloride + potassium sulfate

12. mercury (I) nitrate + nickel sulfate

(continued)

13. phosphoric acid + ammonium hydroxide

14. potassium hydroxide + ammonium bromide

15. copper (II) sulfate + sodium bromide

16. ammonium bromide + calcium hydroxide

17. calcium nitrate + potassium chloride

18. lithium hydroxide + hydrosulfuric acid

19. ferric chloride + sodium sulfide

20. iron (II) acetate + potassium phosphate

21. sodium sulfite + hydrobromic acid

22. ammonium phosphate + magnesium nitrate

23. nickel (II) chloride + sodium carbonate

24. calcium hydroxide + acetic acid

25. zinc chloride + sodium phosphate

(continued)

26. barium carbonate + phosphoric acid

27. nitric acid + strontium hydroxide

28. sulfuric acid + sodium chloride

29. potassium sulfate + ammonium nitrate

30. lead (II) sulfate + sodium bromide

31. zinc chlorate + ammonium sulfide

32. calcium chloride + manganese (II) iodide

33. ammonium sulfate + barium hydroxide

34. potassium iodide + ammonium nitrate

35. mercuric chloride + aluminum bromide

VI. Use ionic equations to show how hydrolysis will occur when each of the following salts is put into water:

1. ammonium chloride

(continued)

2. sodium acetate

3. lithium sulfide

4. ammonium sulfate

5. potassium cyanide

6. rubidium acetate

7. sodium borate

8. ammonium sulfite

9. lithium carbonate

10. ammonium nitrate

11. calcium acetate

12. sodium carbonate

13. ammonium acetate

14. potassium sulfite

15. ammonium bicarbonate

Equilibria

I. Write an equilibrium constant for each of the following reactions.

1. $2\ SO_2 + O_2 \rightleftharpoons 2\ SO_3$

2. $2\ CO + O_2 \rightleftharpoons 2\ CO_2$

3. $N_2 + 3\ H_2 \rightleftharpoons 2\ NH_3$

4. $H_2 + Cl_2 \rightleftharpoons 2\ HCl$

5. $2\ N_2 + O_2 \rightleftharpoons 2\ N_2O$

6. $2\ NO + O_2 \rightleftharpoons 2\ NO_2$

7. $HC_2H_3O_2 \rightleftharpoons H^+ + C_2H_3O_2^-$

8. $HCN \rightleftharpoons H^+ + CN^-$

(continued)

9. $AgCl \rightleftharpoons Ag^{+} + Cl^{-}$

10. $PbI_2 \rightleftharpoons Pb^{2+} + 2\ I^{-}$

11. $Bi_2S_3 \rightleftharpoons 2\ Bi^{3+} + 3\ S^{2-}$

12. $Ca_3(PO_4)_2 \rightleftharpoons 3\ Ca^{2+} + 2\ PO_4^{3-}$

II. In each of the following, determine the unknown quantity from the information given. The number in parentheses refers to the corresponding reaction in Part I to which you should refer.

1. Find K_{eq} if $[SO_2] = 1.0$; $[O_2] = 1.0$; $[SO_3] = 2.0$ (1.)

2. Find K_{eq} if $[CO] = 0.5$; $[O_2] = 0.5$; $[CO_2] = 2.5$ (2.)

3. Find K_{eq} if $[N_2] = 0.25$; $[H_2] = 0.10$; $[NH_3] = 0.010$ (3.)

4. Find K_{eq} if $[H_2] = 2.0 \times 10^{-3}$; $[Cl_2] = 2.5 \times 10^{-2}$; $[HCl] = 1.5 \times 10^{-3}$ (4.)

5. Find $[O_2]$ if $K_{eq} = 45.0$; $[N_2] = 1.0$; $[N_2O] = 1.0$ (5.)

6. Find $[NO]$ if $[O_2] = 0.10$; $[NO_2] = 0.20$; $K_{eq} = 10.0$ (6.)

7. Find $[N_2]$ if $[H_2] = 1.0 \times 10^{-2}$; $[NH_3] = 2.0 \times 10^{-3}$; $K_{eq} = 1.5 \times 10^{-4}$ (3.)

(continued)

8. Find [CO] if $[O_2] = 1.3 \times 10^{-3}$; $[CO_2] = 2.5 \times 10^{-4}$; $K_{eq} = 3.6 \times 10^{-3}$; (2.)

9. Find K_i if $[HC_2H_3O_2] = 0.10$; $[H^+] = [C_2H_3O_2^-] = 0.0010$ (7.)

10. Find K_i if $[HCN] = 0.0010$; $[H^+] = 0.010$; $[CN^-] = 2.0 \times 10^{-8}$ (8.)

11. Find $[C_2H_3O_2^-]$ if $[HC_2H_3O_2] = 1.5 \times 10^{-2}$; $[H^+] = 2.0 \times 10^{-3}$; $K_i = 1.8 \times 10^{-5}$ (7.)

12. Find $[H^+]$ if $[HCN] = 3.6 \times 10^{-3}$ and $[CN^-] = [H^+]$; $K_i = 5.8 \times 10^{-8}$ (8.)

13. Find K_{sp} if the solubility of silver chloride is 4.3×10^{-6} g/100 mL (9.)

14. Find K_{sp} if the solubility of bismuth sulfide is 2.9×10^{-5} g/100 mL (11.)

15. Find $[Pb^{2+}]$ if K_{sp} for PbI_2 is 7.5×10^{-9} (10.)

16. Find the solubility in grams/100 mL of calcium ion if K_{sp} for calcium phosphate is 3.2×10^{-24} (12.)

III. Solve each of the following problems involving equilibria.

1. Calculate the equilibrium constant for the following reaction, $2A + B \rightleftharpoons 3C + D$, where molar concentrations are A = 3; B = 2; C = 2; and D = 4.

2. The equilibrium constant, K, for the reaction $A + B \rightleftharpoons 2C$ is 50. After mixing equimolar quantities of A and B, the equilibrium concentration of C is found to be 0.50. What are the concentrations of A and B at equilibrium?

(continued)

3. Consider the reaction PCl_5 (g) $\rightleftharpoons$ PCl_3 (g) + Cl_2 (g). The equilibrium mixture in a 9.0 L container was found to include 0.25 mol PCl_5, 0.36 mol PCl_3, and 0.36 mol Cl_2. From this data, calculate the equilibrium constant for the dissociation at the reaction temperature of 225° C.

4. Nitrogen is caused to react with hydrogen to form ammonia at 450° C in a 4.0 L vessel. At equilibrium, the partial pressures observed for each of the species in the reaction was as follows: NH_3: 900 mm; N_2: 180 mm; and H_2: 305 mm. From this information, calculate the equilibrium constant for the reaction at this temperature.

5. Consider the reaction $H_2 + I_2 \rightleftharpoons 2HI$. The equilibrium constant for this reaction is 32. If, at equilibrium, the concentration of HI is 0.40 and that of I_2 is 0.05, what is the concentration of H_2?

6. The equilibrium constant for the following reaction is 8.

$$4\ Al\ (s) + 3O_2\ (g) \rightleftharpoons 2Al_2O_3\ (s)$$

What is the concentration of oxygen at equilibrium?

7. For the reaction $H_2 + I_2 \rightleftharpoons 2HI$, what is the equilibrium constant if the following concentrations of substances are observed at equilibrium?

$[H_2] = 5.62$ M

$[HI] = 7.89$ M

$[I_2] = 0.130$ M

8. Given the equilibrium concentrations shown below, what is the dissociation constant for ammonia?

$[NH_3] = 0.0015$ M

$[N_2] = 0.069$ M

$[H_2] = 0.032$ M

9. In a saturated solution of $Ag_2C_2O_4$, the concentration of silver ion is 3.4×10^{-4} mol/L. From this information, compute the solubility product of $Ag_2C_2O_4$.

(continued)

10. What amount of chloride ion must be exceeded before silver chloride will precipitate out of a solution in which the concentration of silver ion is 3.6×10^{-3} mol/L? K_{sp} for AgCl is 1.8×10^{-10} at 25° C.

11. A solution in contact with solid silver chromate contains CrO_4^{-2} ions in the concentration of 0.099 mol/L and Ag^{+1} ions at a concentration of 4.0×10^{-6} mol/L. From this information, what is the value of K_{sp} for silver chromate?

12. K_{sp} for HgS is 3×10^{-53}. If mercury (II) nitrate has a concentration of 1.0×10^{-14} mol/L, what is the maximum amount of sulfide ion that can exist in this solution?

13. Consider the reaction $SrCO_3$ (s) $\rightleftharpoons$ Sr^{2+} + CO_3^{2-}. Given that the molar concentrations of the two ions in this reaction are each 3.07×10^{-5} mol/L, what is the value of K_{sp} for $SrCO_3$?

14. If the solubility product for AgBr is 4.9×10^{-13} at 25° C, and the molar concentrations of Ag^+ and Br^- are each 9.1×10^{-5} mol/L in a solution of AgBr, will there be a precipitate of AgBr formed?

15. Given that K_{sp} for $Ca_3(PO_4)_2$ is 1.0×10^{-26}, what are the molar concentrations of Ca^{2+} and PO_4^{3-} in a saturated solution?

16. The solubility product of $PbCl_2$ at 25° C is 1.6×10^{-5}. If $[Cl^-] = 3.0 \times 10^{-2}$, what is the concentration of lead ion in equilibrium with the chloride ion?

17. **Le Chatelier's Principle**

Predict the effects of (a) an increase in pressure and (b) an increase in temperature on each of the following reactions.

1. $2\ SO_2\ (g) + O_2\ (g) \rightleftharpoons 2\ SO_3\ (g)$
2. $2\ O_3\ (g) \rightleftharpoons 3\ O_2\ (g)$
3. $2\ NO_2\ (g) \rightleftharpoons N_2O_4\ (g)$
4. $CO_2\ (g) + H_2\ (g) \rightleftharpoons CO\ (g) + H_2O\ (g)$
5. $C\ (s) + H_2O\ (g) \rightleftharpoons CO\ (g) + H_2\ (g)$
6. $N_2\ (g) + O_2\ (g) \rightleftharpoons 2\ NO\ (g)$

Acids and Bases

Determine the hydrogen ion concentration ([H^+]), hydroxide ion concentration ([OH^-]), pH and pOH of each of the following solutions. For weak acids and bases, the degree of ionization is given in parentheses.

1. 0.10 M HCl
2. 1.0 M HNO_3
3. 0.10 M NaOH
4. 1.0 M KOH
5. 0.10 M $HC_2H_3O_2$ (1.0%)
6. 0.010 M $HC_2H_3O_2$ (10.0%)
7. 1.0 M $HC_2H_3O_2$ (0.10%)
8. 0.10 M NH_4OH (1.0%)
9. 0.0010 M NH_4OH (10.0%)
10. 0.010 M NH_4OH (1.0%)
11. 0.10 M HCN (0.50%)
12. 0.010 M HCN (1.5%)
13. 1.0×10^{-4} M HCN (3.5%)
14. 0.015 M HCN (1.2%)
15. 0.0038 M HCN (2.3%)
16. 0.0016 M tartaric acid (0.042%)

(continued)

17. 2.1×10^{-4} M tartaric acid (1.5×10^{-2}%)

18. 1.6×10^{-3} M oxalic acid (0.166%)

19. 5.8×10^{-2} M oxalic acid (0.086%)

20. 4.25×10^{-4} M oxalic acid (0.835%)

21. 0.64 M NH_4OH (1.2%)

22. 0.098 M NH_4OH (1.6%)

23. 3.4×10^{-3} M NH_4OH (3.7%)

24. 0.88 M NH_4OH (0.95%)

25. What is the hydrogen ion concentration in a solution containing 0.020 M benzoic acid and 0.010 M sodium benzoate? K_a for benzoic acid is 6.6×10^{-5}, and the acid ionizes as follows:

$$C_6H_5COOH(aq) \rightarrow H^+(aq) + C_6H_5COO^-(aq)$$

26. Calculate the pH of a solution whose hydrogen ion concentration is 0.0036 mol/L.

27. What would be the ionization constant for acetic acid at 25° C if a 0.010 M solution of this acid is ionized to the extent of 1.38%?

28. 30 g of acetic acid is dissolved in enough water to make one liter of solution. What is the molarity of the solution, and what is the hydrogen ion concentration in the solution?

29. What are the $[H^+]$ and $[ClO^-]$ for a 0.048 M solution of HClO? K_i for HClO is 3.5×10^{-8}.

30. What is the pH of a solution of 0.0010 M hydrochloric acid?

31. Calculate the pH of a 0.30 M solution of aniline, $C_6H_5NH_2$. K_b for aniline is 4.2×10^{-10}.

(continued)

32. Complete the equations for each of the following acid-base reactions:

a. $HF(aq) + CH_3COO^-(aq) \rightarrow$

b. $H_2S(aq) + CO_3^{-2}(aq) \rightarrow$

c. $NH_4^+(aq) + F^-(aq) \rightarrow$

33. Define acid equilibrium expressions for each of the following reactions:

a. $HNO_2(aq) + NH_3(aq) \rightarrow NO_2^-(aq) + NH_4^+(aq)$

b. $C_6H_5COOH(aq) + CH_3COO^-(aq) \rightarrow C_6H_5COO^-(aq) + CH_3COOH(aq)$

34. Identify the conjugate acid-base pairs in each of the following reactions.

a. $HSO_4^-(aq) + C_2O_4^{2-}(aq) \rightleftharpoons SO_4^{2-} + HC_2O_4^-(aq)$

b. $H_2PO_4^-(aq) + HCO_3^-(aq) \rightleftharpoons HPO_4^{2-}(ag) + H_2CO_3(aq)$

c. $H_2O + S^{2-}(aq) \rightleftharpoons HS^-(aq) + OH^-(aq)$

d. $CN^-(aq) + HC_2H_3O_2(aq) \rightleftharpoons HCN(aq) + C_2H_3O_2^-(aq)$

e. $HNO_2(aq) + H_2O \rightleftharpoons H_3O^+(aq) + NO_2^-(aq)$

35. Classify each of the following as a Lewis acid or base.

a. H_2O b. O^{2-} c. S^{2-} d. H^+ e. BF_3 f. Cu^{2+}

g. Cl^- h. SO_3 in the reaction: $SO_3 + CaO \rightleftharpoons CaSO_4$

Standard Solutions

• *EQUIVALENT WEIGHT*

I. A. Calculate the equivalent weight of each of the following.

1. oxygen
2. carbon
3. germanium
4. tantalum
5. palladium
6. fluorine
7. aluminum chloride
8. barium iodide
9. sodium fluoride
10. lithium hydroxide
11. calcium nitrate
12. ammonium sulfate

B. Calculate the milliequivalent weight of each of the following. In the case of polyprotic acids, calculate all possible equivalent and milliequivalent weights.

1. sulfuric acid
2. potassium phosphate
3. ferric bromide
4. ammonium nitrite
5. potassium chlorate
6. rubidium hydroxide
7. mercury (II) nitrate
8. phosphoric acid

(continued)

9. cobalt (II) bisulfate
10. ammonium bicarbonate
11. calcium hydroxide
12. cesium chloride

C. **How many equivalent weights are contained in each of the following?**

1. 40.0 g of sodium hydroxide
2. 36.5 g of hydrochloric acid
3. 223.6 g of copper (II) bromide
4. 74 g of calcium hydroxide
5. 50.0 g of calcium carbonate
6. 196 g of sulfuric acid
7. 21 g of nitric acid
8. 133.5 g of aluminum chloride
9. 100. g of potassium bromide
10. 85 g of cadmium nitrate

D. **How many milliequivalent weights are contained in each of the following?**

1. 250. g of aluminum bromide
2. 125 g of ferrous hydroxide
3. 340. g of ammonium chloride
4. 58 g of sodium phosphate
5. 145 g of cadmium sulfate
6. 425 g of aluminum sulfate
7. 60.0 g of nickel (II) chloride
8. 15.0 g of barium acetate
9. 10.0 g of strontium hydroxide
10. 40.0 g of lithium carbonate

• *STANDARD SOLUTIONS*

II. A. Tell how you would prepare each of the following solutions:

1. 1.0 L of 1.0 M potassium chloride
2. 1.0 L of 1.0 M strontium nitrate
3. 1.0 L of 1.0 M sodium sulfate
4. 2.0 L of 1.0 M lithium bromide

(continued)

5. 5.0 L of 1.0 M aluminum nitrate

6. 1.0 L of 0.10 M calcium chloride

7. 1.0 L of 0.10 M beryllium nitrate

8. 1.0 L of 0.20 M sodium nitrate

9. 1.0 L of 0.010 M magnesium hydroxide

10. 500. mL of 0.10 M ammonium carbonate

11. 40.0 mL of 2.0 M rubidium fluoride

12. 600. mL of 0.10 M sodium sulfide

13. 100. mL of 0.20 M aluminum sulfate

14. 250. mL of 0.040 M ammonium chloride

15. 50. mL of 5.0 M potassium phosphate

16. 400. mL of 0.10 M barium nitrate

17. 500. mL of 6.0 M sodium phosphate

18. 25 mL of 0.40 M cesium nitrate

19. 100. mL of 0.50 M mercuric chlorate

20. 750. mL of 6.0 M potassium sulfate

21. 1.0 L of 1.0 N hydrochloric acid

22. 1.0 L of 1.0 N calcium iodide

23. 1.0 L of 1.0 N aluminum chloride

24. 1.0 L of 1.0 N phosphoric acid

(continued)

25. 1.0 L of 2.0 N barium acetate

26. 1.0 L of 2.0 N sodium hydroxide

27. 1.0 L of 2.0 N nickel (II) chloride

28. 1.0 L of 4.0 N aluminum nitrate

29. 1.0 L of 6.0 N nitric acid

30. 1.0 L of 0.10 N zinc chloride

31. 1.0 L of 0.10 N barium hydroxide

32. 1.0 L of 0.10 N cadmium sulfate

33. 1.0 L of 0.10 N hydrobromic acid

34. 1.0 L of 0.20 N copper (II) bromide

35. 1.0 L of 0.20 N magnesium nitrate

36. 1.0 L of 0.010 N rubidium hydroxide

37. 1.0 L of 0.010 N nickel nitrate

38. 1.0 L of 0.010 N strontium hydroxide

39. 1.0 L of 0.020 N bismuth bromide

40. 1.0 L of 0.040 N silver nitrate

41. 2.0 L of 1.0 N aluminum sulfate

42. 4.0 L of 1.0 N cupric nitrate

43. 500. mL of 1.0 N hydrogen iodide

44. 200. mL of 1.0 N iron (II) chloride

(continued)

45. 750 mL of 1.0 N potassium hydroxide

46. 100. mL of 1.0 N mercury (II) chloride

47. 250. mL of 2.0 N cadmium chlorate

48. 300. mL of 0.10 N sulfuric acid

49. 500. mL of 0.10 N calcium chloride

50. 100. mL of 0.10 N nickel sulfate

51. 250. mL of 0.20 N ammonium hydroxide

52. 50.0 mL of 4.0 N iron (III) nitrate

53. 25 mL of 0.80 N aluminum iodide

54. 30.0 mL of 0.010 N lead (II) acetate

55. 200. mL of 0.50 N lithium hydroxide

56. 350. mL of 0.030 N magnesium chloride

57. 150. mL of 0.020 N copper (II) sulfate

58. 50.0 mL of 2.0 N barium nitrate

59. 250. mL of 0.20 N manganese (II) sulfate

60. 8.0 L of 0.10 N cadmium nitrate

B. What is the molarity and normality of each of the following solutions?

1. 40. g of sodium hydroxide in 1.0 L of solution

2. 122.5 g of potassium chlorate in 1.0 L of solution

3. 133.5 g of aluminum chloride in 1.0 L of solution

(continued)

4. 142 g of sodium sulfate in 1.0 L of solution

5. 342 g of aluminum sulfate in 1.0 L of solution

6. 58.5 g sodium chloride in 1.0 L of solution

7. 98 g of sulfuric acid in 0.50 L of solution

8. 21.2 g of lithium chloride in 4.0 L of solution

9. 7.8 g of potassium hydroxide in 500. mL of solution

10. 32.7 g of phosphoric acid in 250. mL of solution

11. 49 g of ammonium bromide in 2.0 L of solution

12. 1.2 g of lithium hydroxide in 100. mL of solution

13. 9.0 g of calcium chloride in 250. mL of solution

14. 20.0 g of nitric acid in 500. mL of solution

15. 12.3 g of aluminum sulfate in 400. mL of solution

16. 1.2 g of hydrochloric acid in 750. mL of solution

17. 4.1 g of manganese (II) chloride in 300. mL of solution

18. 17.2 g of potassium phosphate in 250. mL of solution

19. 6.6 g of barium hydroxide in 50. mL of solution

20. 44.2 g of ammonium sulfate in 600. mL of solution

21. 0.014 g of calcium nitrate in 10.0 mL of solution

22. 0.28 g of hydrobromic acid in 45 mL of solution

23. 4.3 g of sodium nitrite in 100. mL of solution

(continued)

24. 2.9 g of ferric sulfate in 250. mL of solution

25. 0.40 g of strontium hydroxide in 38 mL of solution

• *PERCENT SOLUTIONS*

III. Express the concentration of each of the following solutions in percent weight/volume (w/v), weight/weight (w/w), or volume/volume (v/v) as indicated.

1. 5.0 g in 100.0 mL (w/v)
2. 2.5 g in 100.0 g (w/w)
3. 1.0 mL in 100.0 mL (v/v)
4. 3.0 g in 50.0 mL (w/v)
5. 0.25 g in 25.0 mL (w/v)
6. 1.5 g in 50.0 g (w/w)
7. 0.75 mL in 10.0 mL (v/v)
8. 1.89 g in 30.0 mL (w/v)
9. 0.62 g in 45.0 g (w/w)
10. 15.3 mL in 2.65 L (v/v)
11. 4.5 g in 138.6 mL (w/v)
12. 0.575 g in 265 g (w/w)

IV. What mass of solute is contained in each of the following solutions?

1. 100.0 mL of a 1.5% (w/v) solution
2. 100.0 g of a 2.3% (w/w) solution
3. 50.0 mL of a 2.5% (w/v) solution
4. 25.0 mL of a 0.50% (w/v) solution
5. 75.0 g of a 1.2% (w/w) solution

(continued)

6. 50.0 mL of a 2.8% (w/v) solution
7. 32.5 mL of a 1.8% (w/v) solution
8. 75.0 mL of a 2.6% (w/v) solution
9. 56.5 g of a 1.4% (w/w) solution
10. 11.2 mL of a 0.45% (w/v) solution
11. 1.45 mL of a 0.33% (w/v) solution
12. 2.43 L of a 0.042% (w/v) solution

V. What volume of each of the following solutions would be needed to deliver the stated amount of solute?

1. 1.0 g of a 1.0% (w/v) solution
2. 3.0 g of a 1.5% (w/v) solution
3. 0.5 g of a 1.0% (w/v) solution
4. 1.5 g of a 0.50% (w/v) solution
5. 0.25 g of a 2.0% (w/v) solution
6. 1.0 g of a 0.9% (w/v) solution
7. 2.5 g of a 0.45% (w/v) solution
8. 2.0 mL of a 1.5% (v/v) solution
9. 10.0 mL of a 2.5% (v/v) solution
10. 3.5 mL of a 1.5% (v/v) solution
11. 5.0 g of a 0.9% (w/v) solution
12. 4.2 mL of a 1.3 % (v/v) solution

VI. Calculate the normality of the following solutions from the information given (SG = specific gravity of the solution; % = percentage concentration of the solution):

1. hydrochloric acid: SG = 1.19; % = 36
2. nitric acid: SG = 1.42; % = 69.5
3. sulfuric acid: SG = 1.84; % = 96.0
4. ammonium hydroxide: SG = 0.90; % = 58.6
5. acetic acid: SG = 1.06; % = 99.5
6. cupric sulfate: SG = 1.20; % = 18
7. magnesium chloride: SG = 1.27; % = 30.0
8. nickel (II) nitrate: SG = 1.38; % = 35
9. sodium thiosulfate: SG = 1.30; % = 31.9
10. zinc chloride: SG = 1.96; % = 70.0

VII. If you were given 100. mL of each of the following solutions, how would you make a 0.10 N solution of hydrochloric acid?

1. 1.0 N HCl
2. 6.0 N HCl
3. 5.0 N HCl
4. 2.0 N HCl
5. 2.4 N HCl
6. 3.0 N HCl
7. 10.0 N HCl
8. 0.50 N HCl
9. 0.40 N HCl
10. 1.0 M HCl

VIII. If you were given 100. mL of each of the following solutions, how would you make a 0.0020 N solution of sulfuric acid?

1. 0.10 N H_2SO_4
2. 4.0 N H_2SO_4
3. 36 N H_2SO_4
4. 6.0 N H_2SO_4
5. 0.010 N H_2SO_4
6. 0.50 N H_2SO_4
7. 0.020 N H_2SO_4
8. 2.0 M H_2SO_4
9. 0.20 N H_2SO_4
10. 0.40 M H_2SO_4

• *TITRATIONS*

IX. Solve the following problems:

1. You are given 40.0 mL of 0.10 N hydrochloric acid. What volume of sodium hydroxide is needed to neutralize completely all the acid when the base has the following normalities:

   a. 0.20 N
   b. 0.010 N
   c. 4.0 N
   d. 5.0 N
   e. 0.0020 N
   f. 1.0 N
   g. 0.40 N
   h. 2.0 N
   i. 0.10 N
   j. 0.50 N

2. You are given 50.0 mL of 0.20 N sodium hydroxide. If the following volumes of acid were used to neutralize this base, what was the normality of the acid in each case?

   a. 10.0 mL
   b. 250. mL
   c. 5.0 mL
   d. 100.0 mL

(continued)

e. 40.0 mL

f. 70.0 mL

g. 20.0 mL

h. 62.5 mL

i. 12.5 mL

j. 30.0 mL

3. What volume of 0.50 N sulfuric acid is needed to react completely with 10.0 mL of 2.0 N potassium hydroxide?

4. 25 mL of acetic acid exactly neutralize 30.0 mL of 0.40 N sodium hydroxide. What is the normality of the acetic acid?

5. 23.8 mL of sulfuric acid neutralize 34.2 mL of 0.20 N potassium hydroxide. What is the normality of the sulfuric acid?

6. How many milliliters of 2.0 N sodium hydroxide are needed to neutralize 15 mL of 0.60 N hydrochloric acid?

7. What volume of 0.50 N ammonium hydroxide is required to react completely with 15 mL of 0.2 N hydrochloric acid?

8. 16 mL of 2.0 N sodium hydroxide neutralize 25 mL of hydrochloric acid. What is the normality of the acid?

9. 50.0 mL of 0.010 N acetic acid will neutralize 65.0 mL of potassium hydroxide. What is the normality of the base?

10. How many milliliters of 0.10 N sodium hydroxide are needed to react completely with 26.2 mL of 0.30 N sulfuric acid?

(continued)

11. How many milliliters of 0.10 N hydrochloric acid are needed to react completely with the following?

a. 5.0 g of sodium hydroxide

b. 100.0 mg of calcium hydroxide

c. 12.5 g of potassium hydroxide

d. 2.00 g of lithium hydroxide

e. 10.0 mg of barium hydroxide

f. 30.0 g of sodium hydroxide

g. 6.2 g of potassium hydroxide

h. 15.7 g of barium hydroxide

i. 1.0 g of calcium hydroxide

j. 40.0 mg of strontium hydroxide

12. 50.0 mL of a hydrochloric acid solution are required to react completely with 1.204 g of calcium carbonate. What is the normality of the acid?

13. 42.6 mL of sulfuric acid precipitate exactly 3.260 g of barium sulfate from a solution. What is the normality of the acid?

14. A 0.15 N solution of calcium chloride is added to a solution of ammonium carbonate and 2.010 g of calcium carbonate are precipitated. What volume of chloride solution was added?

15. 3.0 g of silver nitrate are dissolved in water. 36.0 mL of a sodium chloride solution are needed to completely precipitate all the silver chloride from this solution. What was the normality of the sodium chloride solution?

(continued)

16. An excess of hydrogen sulfide gas is passed into 40.0 mL of each of the following solutions: bismuth nitrate, cadmium nitrate, cupric nitrate, ferrous nitrate, ferric nitrate, lead nitrate, manganese nitrate, mercurous nitrate, mercuric nitrate, nickel nitrate, silver nitrate, zinc nitrate. The following amounts of precipitates are formed. What was the normality of the original nitrate solution in each case?

a. Bi_2S_3	3.24 g	g. MnS	0.904 g
b. CdS	0.834 g	h. Hg_2S	3.04 g
c. CuS	0.654 g	i. HgS	2.15 g
d. FeS	0.215 g	j. NiS	0.832 g
e. Fe_2S_3	1.248 g	k. Ag_2S	1.462 g
f. PbS	1.044 g	l. ZnS	0.058 g

• *MOLAL SOLUTIONS*

X. Solve the following problems.

1. How would you make each of the following solutions?
   a. 1.0 m NaCl
   b. 2.0 m H_2SO_4
   c. 0.25 m sucrose ($C_{12}H_{22}O_{11}$)
   d. 500. mL of 1.0 m ethyl alcohol (C_2H_5OH)
   e. 500. mL of 0.50 m H_3PO_4
   f. 1.5 L of 0.25 m nitric acid
   g. 75 mL of 0.30 m sodium hydroxide
   h. 150. mL of 0.500 m ammonium hydroxide
2. What is the molality of each of the following solutions?
   a. 40.0 g of NaOH in 1.00 kg of water.
   b. 45.0 g of glucose ($C_6H_{12}O_6$) in 1.00 kg of water.
   c. 10.0 g of NaCl in 500. g of water.
   d. 30.0 g of sucrose in 125 g of water.
   e. 2.5 g of sulfuric acid in 200. g of water.
   f. 4.5 g of glucose in 200. g of water.
   g. 30.0 g of phosphoric acid in 250. g of water.
   h. 41 g of calcium chloride in 300. mL of water.

Colligative Properties

Solve the following problems:

1. What is the boiling point of a solution that consists of 1.0 mol of sucrose ($C_{12}H_{22}O_{11}$) dissolved in 1.0 kg of water?

2. What is the freezing point of a solution that contains 0.50 mol of sucrose dissolved in 1.0 kg of water?

3. What is the boiling point of a solution that consists of 171 g of sucrose in 2.0 kg of water?

4. What is the freezing point of a solution that contains 34.2 g of sucrose in 250 g of water?

5. What is the boiling point of a solution that consists of 15.0 g of sucrose in 150. g of water?

6. What is the freezing point of a solution that contains 10.0 g of sucrose in 85.0 g of water?

7. 3.7 g of hexanoyl chloride ($C_6H_{11}OCl$) are dissolved in 50.0 g of benzene. What is the freezing point of this solution?

8. What is the freezing point of a solution that contains 4.50 g of p-cresyl acetate ($C_9H_{10}O_2$) dissolved in 50.0 g of benzene?

9. 40.0 g of an organic compound dissolved in 1.00 kg of water have a boiling point of 100.52° C. What is the molecular weight of the solute?

10. 35.0 g of an organic compound dissolved in 500. g of water have a freezing point of −3.72° C. What is the molecular weight of the solute?

(continued)

11. 63.2 g of an organic compound dissolved in 350. g of water have a boiling point of 101.5° C. What is the molecular weight of the solute?

12. 5.85 g of an organic compound dissolved in 75.0 g of water have a freezing point of −1.04° C. What is the molecular weight of the compound?

13. 3.33 g of an organic compound dissolved in 150. g of carbon tetrachloride have a boiling point of 78.5° C. What is the molecular weight of this compound?

14. 1.43 g of an organic solute dissolved in 50.0 g of benzene have a freezing point of 4.2° C. What is the molecular weight of the solute?

15. An organic compound whose molecular weight is 140 is dissolved in 1000 g of cyclohexane. The freezing point of the solution is 4.75° C. How much of the compound was dissolved in the cyclohexane?

Redox Reactions

Balance the following redox reactions:

1. $H_2SO_3 + I_2 + H_2O \rightarrow H_2SO_4 + HI$

2. $FeCl_3 + SnCl_2 \rightarrow FeCl_2 + SnCl_4$

3. $SbCl_5 + KI \rightarrow SbCl_3 + KCl + I_2$

4. $CdS + I_2 + HCl \rightarrow CdCl_2 + HI + S$

5. $KClO_3 + FeSO_4 + H_2SO_4 \rightarrow KCl + Fe_2(SO_4)_3 + H_2O$

6. $CuSO_4 + KI \rightarrow CuI + K_2SO_4 + I_2$

7. $AuCl_3 + KI \rightarrow AuCl + KCl + I_2$

8. $SnCl_2 + HgCl_2 \rightarrow SnCl_4 + HgCl$

9. $Ti_2(SO_4)_3 + Fe_2(SO_4)_3 \rightarrow Ti(SO_4)_2 + FeSO_4$

10. $NaClO + H_2S \rightarrow NaCl + H_2SO_4$

11. $Fe_3O_4 + KMnO_4 + H_2SO_4 \rightarrow Fe_2(SO_4)_3 + K_2SO_4 + MnSO_4 + H_2O$

12. $NaCrO_2 + NaOH + H_2O_2 \rightarrow Na_2CrO_4 + H_2O$

13. $Ag + HNO_3 \rightarrow AgNO_3 + NO + H_2O$

14. $Ag_2S + HNO_3 \rightarrow AgNO_3 + NO + S + H_2O$

(continued)

15. $FeS + HNO_3 \rightarrow Fe(NO_3)_3 + NO + S + H_2O$

16. $AgNO_3 + NaClO \rightarrow AgCl + AgClO_3 + NaNO_3$

17. $Ca(OH)_2 + Cl_2 \rightarrow CaCl_2 + Ca(ClO_3)_2 + H_2O$

18. $MnO_2 + FeSO_4 + H_2SO_4 \rightarrow MnSO_4 + Fe_2(SO_4)_3 + H_2O$

19. $I_2 + Na_2S_2O_3 \rightarrow Na_2S_4O_6 + NaI$

20. $Bi(NO_3)_3 + Al + NaOH \rightarrow Bi + NH_3 + NaAlO_2$

21. $Cu_2As_2O_7 + Zn + H_2SO_4 \rightarrow Cu + AsH_3 + ZnSO_4 + H_2O$

22. $FeCl_2 + HCl + HNO_3 \rightarrow FeCl_3 + NO + H_2O$

23. $PbCrO_4 + HCl \rightarrow PbCl_2 + CrCl_3 + Cl_2 + H_2O$

24. $K_2Cr_2O_7 + HCl + H_2S \rightarrow KCl + CrCl_3 + S + H_2O$

25. $Ag + HNO_3 + Ca(ClO)_2 \rightarrow AgCl + Ca(NO_3)_2 + H_2O$

26. $HgS + HCl + HNO_3 \rightarrow HgCl_2 + S + NO + H_2O$

27. $Na_2Cr_2O_7 + HNO_3 + H_2O_2 \rightarrow H_3CrO_8 + NaNO_3 + H_2O$

28. $K_2MnO_4 + HNO_3 \rightarrow KMnO_4 + MnO_2 + KNO_3 + H_2O$

29. $KMnO_4 + NaNO_2 + HCl \rightarrow KCl + MnCl_2 + NaNO_3 + H_2O$

30. $MnCl_2 + NaOH + Br_2 \rightarrow MnO_2 + NaCl + NaBr + H_2O$

(continued)

31. $MnO_2 + HNO_3 + H_2O_2 \rightarrow Mn(NO_3)_2 + O_2 + H_2O$

32. $Mn(NO_3)_2 + KIO_4 + H_2O \rightarrow HMnO_4 + KIO_3 + HNO_3$

33. $Mn(NO_3)_2 + Pb_3O_4 + HNO_3 \rightarrow HMnO_4 + Pb(NO_3)_2 + H_2O$

34. $HMnO_4 + HNO_3 \rightarrow Mn(NO_3)_2 + H_2O + O_2$

35. $Cu(AsO_2)_2 + HCl + HNO_3 + H_2O \rightarrow CuCl_2 + H_2AsO_4 + NO$

36. $H_2C_2O_4 + Ce(SO_4)_2 \rightarrow CO_2 + H_2SO_4 + Ce_2(SO_4)_3$

37. $Cl_2 + AgNO_3 + H_2O \rightarrow AgCl + HClO_3 + HNO_3$

38. $CoSO_4 + KI + KIO_3 + H_2O \rightarrow Co(OH)_2 + K_2SO_4 + I_2$

39. $Fe_3O_4 + HNO_3 \rightarrow Fe(NO_3)_3 + NO + H_2O$

40. $Hg_2I_2 + HCl + HNO_3 \rightarrow HgCl_2 + HIO_3 + NO + H_2O$

41. $ZnI_2 + K_2S_2O_8 \rightarrow I_2 + ZnSO_4 + K_2SO_4$

42. $Mn(NO_3)_2 + HNO_3 + NaBiO_3 \rightarrow HMnO_4 + NaNO_3 + Bi(NO_3)_3 + H_2O$

43. $FeS_2 + Na_2O_2 \rightarrow Fe_2O_3 + Na_2SO_4 + Na_2O$

44. $H_2O_2 + Ce(SO_4)_2 \rightarrow Ce_2 (SO_4)_3 + H_2SO_4 + O_2$

45. $CoCl_2 + HgO + KMnO_4 + H_2O \rightarrow Co(OH)_3 + HgCl_2 + MnO_2 + KCl + H_2O$

46. $UO_2(NO_3)_2 + KI + KIO_3 + H_2O \rightarrow UO_2(OH)_2 + KNO_3 + I_2$

(continued)

47. $V_2O_5 + KI + HCl \rightarrow V_2O_4 + KCl + I_2 + H_2O$

48. $Ca(IO_3)_2 + KI + HCl \rightarrow CaCl_2 + KCl + I_2 + H_2O$

49. $PbO_2 + H_2O_2 + HNO_3 \rightarrow Pb(NO_3)_2 + H_2O + O_2$

50. $CaCl_2O + KI + HCl \rightarrow CaCl_2 + KCl + I_2 + H_2O$

51. $Sn + HNO_3 + H_2O \rightarrow H_2SnO_3 + NO$

52. $Mn(NO_3)_2 + Ca(ClO)_2 + NaOH \rightarrow NaMnO_4 + NaNO_3 + CaCl_2 + H_2O$

53. $KBr + Fe_2(SO_4)_3 \rightarrow Br_2 + K_2SO_4 + FeSO_4$

54. $Sb_2S_5 + HCl + HNO_3 \rightarrow SbCl_5 + S + NO + H_2O$

55. $KMnO_4 + HCl \rightarrow KCl + MnCl_2 + Cl_2 + H_2O$

56. $As + HNO_3 + H_2O \rightarrow H_3AsO_4 + NO$

57. $As_2S_5 + HNO_3 + H_2O \rightarrow H_3AsO_4 + S + NO$

58. $Sb_2S_5 + HCl \rightarrow SbCl_3 + S + H_2S$

59. $CaCl_2O + NaAsO_2 + NaOH \rightarrow CaCl_2 + Na_3AsO_4 + H_2O$

60. $MoO_3 + Zn + H_2SO_4 \rightarrow Mo_2O_3 + ZnSO_4 + H_2O$

61. $KIO_3 + H_2 \rightarrow KI + H_2O$

62. $Na_2Cr_2O_7 + S \rightarrow Na_2SO_4 + Cr_2O_3$

(continued)

63. $ZnSO_4 + KI + KIO_3 + H_2O \rightarrow Zn_5(OH)_8SO_4 + K_2SO_4 + I_2$

64. $MnO_2 + KOH + O_2 \rightarrow K_2MnO_4 + H_2O$

65. $MoO_3 + KI + HCl \rightarrow MoO_2I + KCl + I_2 + H_2O$

66. $K_2SeO_3 + KI + HCl \rightarrow KCl + Se + I_2 + H_2O$

67. $SbCl_3 + I_2 + HCl \rightarrow SbCl_5 + HI$

68. $KIO_3 + KI + HCl \rightarrow KCl + I_2 + H_2O$

69. $HI + HClO_3 \rightarrow HCl + I_2 + H_2O$

70. $FeCl_2 + K_2Cr_2O_7 + HCl \rightarrow FeCl_3 + KCl + CrCl_3 + H_2O$

71. $Sb_2(SO_4)_3 + KMnO_4 + H_2O \rightarrow H_3SbO_4 + K_2SO_4 + MnSO_4 + H_2SO_4$

72. $Ba(BrO_3)_2 + H_3AsO_3 \rightarrow BaBr_2 + H_3AsO_4$

73. $Cr_2(SO_4)_3 + KMnO_4 + H_2O \rightarrow H_2CrO_4 + MnSO_4 + K_2SO_4 + H_2SO_4$

74. $NaAsO_2 + I_2 + H_2O \rightarrow NaAsO_3 + HI$

75. $HBO_2 + KIO_3 + KI \rightarrow KBO_2 + H_2O + I_2$

76. $Al_2(SO_4)_3 + KI + KIO_3 + H_2O \rightarrow Al(OH)_3 + K_2SO_4 + I_2$

77. $HAsO_2 + Ce(SO_4)_2 + H_2O \rightarrow H_3AsO_4 + Ce_2(SO_4)_3 + H_2SO_4$

78. $HNO_3 + H_2S \rightarrow S + NO + H_2O$

(continued)

79. $H_2C_2O_4 + KMnO_4 + HNO_3 \rightarrow CO_2 + Mn(NO_3)_2 + KNO_3 + H_2O$

80. $I_2 + KIO_3 + HCl \rightarrow KCl + ICl + H_2O$

81. $HSbO_2 + KBrO_3 + H_2O \rightarrow H_3SbO_4 + KBr$

82. $Co_2O_3 + HCl \rightarrow CoCl_2 + Cl_2 + H_2O$

83. $CuI + HNO_3 \rightarrow Cu(NO_3)_2 + I_2 + NO + H_2O$

84. $NiS + HNO_3 \rightarrow Ni(NO_3)_2 + NO + S + H_2O$

Nuclear Chemistry

I. Complete the following nuclear reactions:

1. $^{27}_{13}Al + ^{4}_{2}He \rightarrow ^{30}_{15}P +$ ______________

2. $^{63}_{29}Cu + ^{2}_{1}H \rightarrow 2^{1}_{0}n +$ ______________

3. $^{44}_{20}Ca + ^{1}_{1}H \rightarrow ^{44}_{21}Sc +$ ______________

4. $^{9}_{4}Be + ^{4}_{2}He \rightarrow ^{12}_{6}C +$ ______________

5. $^{31}_{15}P + ^{2}_{1}H \rightarrow ^{32}_{15}P +$ ______________

6. $^{37}_{17}Cl +$ ______________ $\rightarrow ^{35}_{16}S + ^{4}_{2}He$

7. $^{30}_{15}P +$ ______________ $\rightarrow ^{30}_{14}Si + ^{1}_{1}H$

8. $^{2}_{1}H + ^{2}_{1}H \rightarrow ^{1}_{1}H +$ ______________

9. $^{11}_{5}B + ^{4}_{2}He \rightarrow ^{14}_{7}N +$ ______________

10. $^{63}_{29}Cu + ^{2}_{1}H \rightarrow ^{64}_{30}Zn +$ ______________

11. $^{2}_{1}H +$ ______________ $\rightarrow ^{1}_{1}H + ^{1}_{0}n$

12. $^{31}_{15}P + ^{1}_{1}H \rightarrow ^{28}_{14}Si +$ ______________

13. $^{14}_{7}N +$ ______________ $\rightarrow ^{17}_{8}O + ^{1}_{1}H$

14. $^{239}_{94}Pu + ^{4}_{2}He \rightarrow ^{1}_{0}n +$ ______________

(continued)

15. $^{63}_{29}Cu + ^{1}_{1}H \rightarrow ^{38}_{17}Cl + ^{1}_{0}n +$ ________________

16. $^{63}_{29}Cu + ^{2}_{1}H \rightarrow ^{64}_{29}Cu +$ ________________

17. $^{235}_{92}U + ^{1}_{0}n \rightarrow ^{95}_{42}Mo + 2^{1}_{0}n +$ ________________

18. $^{6}_{3}Li + ^{2}_{1}H \rightarrow ^{7}_{4}Be +$ ________________

19. $^{3}_{1}H \rightarrow ^{3}_{2}He +$ ________________

20. $^{6}_{3}Li + ^{1}_{0}n \rightarrow ^{4}_{2}He +$ ________________

21. $^{122}_{51}Sb + ^{1}_{0}n \rightarrow ^{122}_{51}Sb +$ ________________

22. $^{214}_{82}Pb \rightarrow ^{0}_{-1}e +$ ________________

23. $^{63}_{29}Cu + ^{2}_{1}H \rightarrow ^{3}_{1}H +$ ________________

24. $^{14}_{7}N +$ ________________ $\rightarrow ^{14}_{6}C + ^{1}_{1}H$

25. $^{6}_{3}Li + ^{1}_{1}H \rightarrow ^{4}_{2}He +$ ________________

26. ________________ $\rightarrow ^{237}_{93}Np + \alpha$

27. $^{2}_{1}H + ^{2}_{1}H \rightarrow ^{3}_{2}He +$ ________________

28. $^{28}_{14}Si + ^{2}_{1}H \rightarrow ^{29}_{14}Si +$ ________________

29. $^{9}_{4}Be + ^{4}_{2}He \rightarrow ^{6}_{3}Li +$ ________________

30. $^{59}_{27}Co + ^{1}_{0}n \rightarrow ^{60}_{27}Co +$ ________________

(continued)

31. $^{63}_{29}Cu + ^{2}_{1}H \rightarrow ^{61}_{28}Ni +$ ________________

32. $^{40}_{18}Ar + ^{2}_{1}H \rightarrow ^{41}_{18}Ar +$ ________________

33. $^{6}_{3}Li + ^{2}_{1}H \rightarrow ^{1}_{0}n + ^{3}_{2}He +$ ________________

34. $^{29}_{14}Si + ^{2}_{1}H \rightarrow ^{1}_{0}n +$ ________________

35. $^{11}_{5}B + ^{1}_{1}H \rightarrow 3X$ (X = ?) ________________

II. Write out in longhand (as in the previous examples) and complete the following nuclear reactions:

1. Li^{6} (p, γ)

2. N^{14} (n, p)

3. Na^{23} (α,) Mg^{26}

4. Cr^{54} (, n) Mn^{54}

5. C^{12} (p, γ)

6. Te^{125} (p, n)

7. B^{10} (, n) N^{13}

8. P^{31} (γ, n)

9. Al^{27} (n, p)

10. Li^{7} (p, n)

III. Suggest a method by which each of the following isotopes can be produced, given the specified conditions (i.p. = incident particle; t = target nucleus):

1. $^{154}_{63}Eu$ (t = $^{152}_{62}Sm$)

2. $^{18}_{9}F$ (i.p. = p)

3. $^{46}_{21}Sc$ (i.p. = n)

4. $^{97}_{43}Tc$ (i.p. = α)

5. $^{95}_{41}Nb$ (t = $^{94}_{40}Zr$)

6. $^{85}_{36}Kr$ (i.p. = d)

7. $^{142}_{59}Pr$ (t = $^{142}_{58}Ce$)

8. $^{90}_{39}Y$ (t = $^{88}_{38}Sr$)

9. $^{103}_{46}Pd$ (i.p. = α)

10. $^{199}_{79}Au$ (t = $^{195}_{78}Pt$)

IV. In the following problems, an original sample of mass m_0 decays over time, t, to a mass of m_t. The half life of the isotope is given as $t_{1/2}$. In each problem, calculate the value of the missing variable.

1. m_0 = 64 g; t = 4 half lives; m_t = ?

2. m_0 = 32 g; t = 8.0 yr; $t_{1/2}$ = 2.0 yr; m_t = ?

(continued)

3. m_0 = 128 g; t = 5 d; $t_{1/2}$ = 24 hr; m_t = ?

4. m_0 = 50.0 g; t = 8.0 min; $t_{1/2}$ = 1.6 min; m_t = ?

5. m_0 = 30.0 g; t = 9840 yr; $t_{1/2}$ = 2460 yr; m_t = ?

6. m_0 = 60.0 g; m_t = 3.8 g; $t_{1/2}$ = 4.3×10^6 yr; t = ?

7. m_0 = 400.0 g; m_t = 50.0 g; $t_{1/2}$ = 13.6 d; t = ?

8. m_0 = 1.0000 g; m_t = 0.15625 g; $t_{1/2}$ = 2325 yr; t = ?

9. m_t = 1.00 g; $t_{1/2}$ = 10.0 min; t = 40.0 min; m_0 = ?

10. m_t = 2.5 g; t = 16.2 yr; $t_{1/2}$ = 3.24 yr; m_0 = ?

11. m_0 = 64.0 g; m_t = 1.0 g; t = 18 min; $t_{1/2}$ = ?

12. m_0 = 18.00 g; m_t = 0.562 g; t = 12.5 d; $t_{1/2}$ = ?

Organic Chemistry

I. Identify the structural group in each of the following compounds and tell which organic family the compound belongs to.

1. $CH_3CH_2CH_3$

2. CH_3CH_2OH

3. $CH_3{-}C(=O)H$

```
          O
         //
CH3–C
         \
          H
```

4. $CH_3CH(CH_3)CH_2CH_3$

5. $CH_3CH_2CH_2CHO$

6. CH_3OCH_3

7. $CH_3{-}C({=}O){-}CH_2CH_3$

```
CH3—C—CH2CH3
        ||
        O
```

8. $CH_2{=}CHCH_2CH_3$

9. $CH_3CHClCH_2CH_3$

10. CH_3CH_2COOH

11. $CH_3COCH_2CH_2CH_2CH_3$

12. $CH_3CH_2CH_2C(=O)OH$

```
                     O
                    //
CH3CH2CH2C
                    \
                     OH
```

(continued)

13. $CH_3C \equiv CH$

14. $CH_2NH_2CH_2CH_3$

15. $CH_3CCl_2CH_3$

II. Write an expanded structural formula for each of the following compounds, and then name the compound.

1. $CH_3CH_2CH_2CH_2CH_2CH_3$

2. $CH_3CH_2CH(CH_3)CH_2CH_2CH_2CH_3$

3. $CH_3CH(CH_3)CH_2CH(CH_3)CH_2CH_3$

4. $CH_3CH_2CH_2CH(C_2H_5)CH_2CH_2CH_3$

5. $CH_3CH(CH_3)C(CH_3)(C_2H_5)CH_2CH_2CH_3$

6. $CH_3CH_2CH_2CH_3$

7. $CH_3CH_2CH(C_2H_5)CH_2CH_3$

8. $CH_3CH_2CH(C_2H_5)CH_2CH_2CH(CH_3)CH_3$

9. $CH_3CH_2CH_2CH(CH_3)CH(CH_3)CH(CH_3)CH_3$

(continued)

10. $CH_3CHBrCH_2CH(CH_3)CH_2CH_3$

11. $CH_3CH_2CH(CH_3)CH(CH_3)CH(C_2H_5)CH_2CH_3$

12. $CH_3CHClCCl(C_2H_5)CH_2CH(CH_3)CH_3$

13. $CH_3CH_2CH_2CH(C_2H_5)C(CH_3)(C_2H_5)CH_2CH_2CH_3$

14. $CH_3CH_2CH_2CHClCHClCH_2CH_2CH(CH_3)CH_3$

15. $CH_2ClCHBrCH_2CH(CH_3)CH_2CH_2CHBrCH_3$

16. $CH_3CH(CH_3)CH_2CH(n{-}C_3H_7)CH(C_2H_5)CH_2CHClCH_3$

17. $CH_3CH_2CH_2CH_2CH(C_2H_5)CH_2CHBrCH_2CH_3$

18. $CH_2ICH_2CH_2CHICH_2CHICH_2CH_3$

19. $CH_3CH_2CHFCH_2CH(CH_3)CHICH_2CH_3$

20. $CH_3CH(CH_3)CH_2CH(C_2H_5)CH_2CHICH_2CH_2CH_3$

21. $CH_2{=}CH_2$

22. $CH_3CH_2CH_2CH{=}CHCH_2CH_3$

(continued)

23. $CH_3CH(CH_3)C(CH_3){=}CHCH_2CH_3$

24. $CH_2{=}CHCH_2CH(CH_3)CHClCH_3$

25. $CH_3CH_2CHBrCH_2CH(CH_3)CH{=}CHCH_3$

26. $CH_3CH{=}CHCH_2CH(CH_3)CH(CH_3)CH_3$

27. $CH_3CH(CH_3)CH{=}C(C_2H_5)CH_2CH_2CH_2Cl$

28. $CH_3CH{=}C(CH_3)CH_2CH_2CHClCH_2Cl$

29. $CH_3CH_2CH{=}CHCH_2CHClCH_2CH_3$

30. $CH_3CH{=}CHC(CH_3)_2CH_2CHClC(CH_3)_2CH_2CH_3$

31. $CH_3CH{=}CHCH_2CCl_2CH_2CH_2Br$

32. $CH_3CH_2CH{=}C(C_2H_5)CH_2CH_2CH_3$

33. $CH_3CHBrCH{=}CBrCH_2CH(CH_3)CH_3$

34. $CH_3CH_2CH{=}C(CH_3)CHBrCH_2CH_2Br$

35. $CH_3CH_2CH{=}CHCHBrCH_2CHClCH_2Cl$

(continued)

36. $CH_3C{\equiv}CH$

37. $CH_3C{\equiv}CCH_3$

38. $CH_3CH_2C{\equiv}CCH_2Br$

39. $CH_3CH(CH_3)CH_2C{\equiv}CCH_3$

40. $CH_3CH_2CH_2C{\equiv}CCH(CH_3)CHBrCH_3$

41. $CH_3CH_2CH_2CH_2OH$

42. $CH_3CH_2CH_2OH$

43. $CH_3CHOHCH_2CH_2CH_3$

44. $CH_3CH_2CHOHCH_3$

45. $CH_3CH_2CH_2CHOHCH_2CH_2CH_3$

46. $CH_3CHOHCH_2CH_2CH_2CH_2CH_3$

47. $CH_3CH_2CHOHCHClCH_3$

48. $CH_3CH_2CH(CH_3)CH_2OH$

(continued)

49. $CH_3CHOHCH(CH_3)CH_2CH_3$

50. $CH_3CH(CH_3)CH_2CH(CH_3)CHOHCH_3$

51. $CH_3C(CH_3)_2CH_2CHOHCH_2CH(CH_3)CH_3$

52. $CH_2OHCH_2CH_2CHClCH(CH_3)CH_3$

53. $CH_3CH(CH_3)CHOHCHClCH_2Cl$

54. $CH_3CH_2CH_2CHOHCH(CH_3)CH(CH_3)CH_3$

55. $CH_2ClCHOHCHClCH_3$

56. $CH_3CHOHCH_2CH_2C(C_2H_5)_2CH_2CH_3$

57. $CH_3CHOHCH_2CHClCH_2CHBrCH_2Cl$

58. $CH_2OHCH(CH_3)CH(C_2H_5)CH_2CH_2CH_3$

59. $CH_2OHCH_2CH_2CH_2OH$

60. $CH_3CH_2CHOHCH_2CH_2CH_2OH$

61. CH_3CHO

(continued)

62. $CH_3CH_2\overset{O}{\overset{\|}{C}}CH_2CH_2CH_3$

63. $CH_3CH_2CH_2CHO$

64. $CH_3CH(CH_3)CH_2CHO$

65. $CH_3CH_2C(CH_3)_2CH_2CHO$

66. $CH_3CH_2CHClCH_2CHO$

67. $C(CH_3)_3CH_2CH(CH_3)CHO$

68. $C(CH_3)_3CH_2CH_2CHO$

69. $CH_3CH_2\overset{O}{\overset{\|}{C}}CH_2CH_2CH_2CH_2CH_3$

70. $CH_3CH_2CH_2\overset{O}{\overset{\|}{C}}CH_2CH(CH_3)CH_3$

71. $CH_3C(CH_3)_2CH_2\overset{O}{\overset{\|}{C}}CH_2CH_3$

72. $CH_3CHClCH_2CH_2CHClCH_2CHO$

(continued)

73. $CH_3\overset{\overset{O}{\|}}{C}CH_2CH_2CHICH_2CH(CH_3)_2$

74. $CH_3CHICH_2CH_2CHICHO$

75. $CH_3C(CH_3)_2CH_2CHI\overset{\overset{O}{\|}}{C}CH_2CH_3$

76. $CH(CH_3)_2CH_2CH_2\overset{\overset{O}{\|}}{C}CH_2CH_2CH_2Br$

77. $CH_3CH_2\overset{\overset{O}{\|}}{C}CH_2CCl_2CH_2CH_2Cl$

78. $CH_3CH_2CH_2CH(CH_3)CH_2CHO$

79. $CH_3C(CH_3)_2CH_2CH_2\overset{\overset{O}{\|}}{C}CH_2CH_2CH_2Cl$

80. $CH_3CH_2CHClCH_2C(CH_3)_2CH_2CHO$

81. CH_3OCH_3

82. $CH_3CH_2OCH_3$

83. $CH_3CH_2CH_2OCH_3$

(continued)

84. $CH_3OCH_2CH_2CH_2CH_2CH_3$

85. $CH_3CH_2OC(CH_3)_3$

86. $CH_3CH_2CH_2COOH$

87. $CH_3CH_2CH_2CH_2COOH$

88. $CH_3CH_2C(CH_3)_2COOH$

89. $CH_3CH(CH_3)CH_2COOH$

90. $HOOCCH_2CH_2COOH$

91. $CH_3CH_2CH(CH_3)CH_2CH_2COOH$

92. $CH_3CH(CH_3)CH_2CH(CH_3)COOH$

93. $CH_3CH_2CH_2CHClCH_2COOH$

94. $CH_3CH_2CHFCH_2CH_2COOH$

95. $CH_3CH_2CHNH_2COOH$

96. $CH_3CH_2CHBrCOOH$

(continued)

97. $CH_3CHBrCH_2CHBrCOOH$

98. $CH_3CH_2CH_2CHNH_2COOH$

99. $CH_3CHOHCH_2COOH$

100. $CH_3CH_2CH_2CH_2CHOHCOOH$

III. Draw structural formulas for each of the following compounds.

1. **n-butane**

2. **2-chloropentane**

3. **3-methylhexane**

4. **n-heptane**

5. **2, 2, 4-trimethylheptane**

6. 4-chloro-2, 3-dimethyloctane

7. 1, 2, 4-trichloropentane

8. 2, 3, 4-trimethylhexane

(continued)

9. 2, 3, 3-trimethylheptane

10. 4-bromo-4-chloro-2-methyldecane

11. 2, 3-dimethyl-3-hexene

12. 2-chloro-1-pentene

13. 3-octene

14. 4-ethyl-2, 3-dimethyl-3-nonene

15. 2, 2, 3, 5-tetramethyl-3-octene

16. 1, 4, 5-tribromo-2, 2-dichloro-3-heptene

17. 3-chloro-2, 3-difluoro-1-butene

18. 1, 3-butadiene

19. ethanol

20. 2-propanol

21. 2-pentanol

(continued)

22. 3, 3-dimethyl-2-hexanol

23. 1, 2, 3-trichloro-1-butanol

24. 3-ethyl-2, 2-dimethyl-1-hexanol

25. 2, 4, 4-trimethyl-2-heptanol

26. 2-bromo-1, 3, 6, 7-tetrachloro-4, 4-dimethyl-1-decanol

27. 1, 3-butanediol

28. 2, 2-dibromo-3, 4-dimethyl-3-hexanol

29. 1, 4-difluoro-2, 2, 3-trimethyl-3-heptanol

30. 3-ethyl-2, 4-diiodo-2, 4, 5-trimethyl-1-nonanol

31. heptanal

32. butyraldehyde

33. methylpropyl ketone

34. diethyl ketone

(continued)

35. 4-nonanone

36. 3-ethyl-2-methylhexanal

37. 3-bromo-2, 2-dichlorobutanal

38. 2-chloro-2, 4-dimethyl-3-hexanone

39. methanal

40. 2, 3, 3-trimethylpentanal

41. 2, 4, 4-trimethyl-3-heptanone

42. 4-chloro-4-iodo-3, 3-dimethyl-2-pentanone

43. 2, 3-dibromo-4, 6, 7-trichlorodecanal

44. 5, 7-diethyl-2, 3, 5-trimethyl-4-nonanone

45. butanoic acid

46. 1, 5-pentanedioic acid

47. α-aminopropionic acid

(continued)

48. 2, 3-dichlorobutanoic acid

49. 3, 3-dimethylhexanoic acid

50. γ-hydroxyvaleric acid

51. 2, 3, 4-tribromodecanoic acid

52. 4, 4, 5-triiodo-2-methylhexanoic acid

53. α-hydroxybutanoic acid

54. 1, 4-butanedioic acid

55. β-hydroxyvaleric acid

56. 4-chloro-2, 3-dimethylhexanoic acid

57. 3, 4-dibromo-2, 5, 7-trichlorodecanoic acid

58. 2, 2-diaminobutanoic acid

59. 5, 6-dichlorooctanoic acid

60. 2, 4-dihydroxypentanoic acid

IV. Write equations, using structural formulas, for the following organic reactions. Include catalysts or special conditions that may be necessary for each reaction to occur.

1. methane + chlorine (in four steps) →

2. propene + chlorine →

3. ethylene (polymerized) →

4. ethyl chloride + sodium hydroxide →

5. hexanal + hydrogen →

6. ethane + bromine →

7. 3-hexene + hydrogen chloride →

8. 2-butene + hydrogen →

9. glyceryl tristearate (hydrolyzed) →

10. benzene + chlorine →

11. 2-butanol + sulfuric acid →

12. octane + oxygen (high temperature) →

(continued)

13. 2-pentanone + hydrogen cyanide →

14. 1-butanol + sodium →

15. n-butane + bromine →

16. acetylene + hydrogen chloride →

17. 1-butene + chlorine →

18. propene (polymerized) →

19. benzene + bromine (in two steps) →

20. methanoic acid + 3-hexanol →

21. 1-propanol + phosphorus trichloride →

22. 1-pentene + hydrogen bromide →

23. n-dodecane + oxygen (high temperature) →

24. toluene + bromine →

25. 2-octene + butane →

(continued)

26. propane + chlorine →

27. 1-butene + hydrogen →

28. 2-octanol + nitric acid →

29. 2-pentene + hydrogen cyanide →

30. 2-butanol + oxygen (mild conditions) →

31. 1-butene (polymerized) →

32. propyne + bromine →

33. n-pentane + bromine →

34. 2-pentanol + sodium →

35. 2-hexene + propane →

36. isopropyl alcohol + butyric acid →

37. 2-pentene + bromine →

38. 3-hexanol + phosphorus trichloride →

(continued)

39. n-octadecane + oxygen (high temperature) →

40. butene + ethane →

41. pentanoic acid + n-butanol →

42. 3-hexanone + hydrogen cyanide →

43. 3-hexanol + oxygen (mild conditions) →

44. glyceryl palmitate distearate (hydrolyzed) →

45. ethanol + ethanoic acid →

46. alanine (α-aminopropionic acid) (polymerized) →

47. glyceryl trilaurate (hydrolyzed) →

48. ethanol + potassium →

49. 2-butanol + propanoic acid →

50. 1-butyne + hydrogen cyanide →

51. benzene (completely chlorinated) →

(continued)

52. glycine (aminoacetic acid) (polymerized) →

53. 2-methylbutane + bromine →

54. glycine + alanine →

55. 2-hexanol + hydrogen chloride →

56. butanal + hydrogen cyanide →

57. toluene + nitric acid →

58. butyric acid + butyl alcohol →

59. hexanal (oxidized) →

60. 2-methyl-1-pentene + bromine →

61. phenol + sodium hydroxide →

62. formaldehyde + ammonia →

63. glycerine + butyric acid →

64. phenol + formaldehyde →

(continued)

65. pentanal + hydrogen chloride →

66. 2-hexene + hydrogen chloride →

67. benzene + sulfuric acid →

68. t-butyl alcohol + phosphorus trichloride →

69. 3-pentanone + hydrogen →

70. methyl alcohol + potassium →

71. propanal + hydrogen →

72. hexane + bromine →

73. benzene + nitric acid (in two steps) →

74. butanal + oxygen (mild conditions) →

75. n-octane + fluorine →

Quantum Mechanics

I. This series of questions deals with the wavelength (λ), frequency (f), and energy (E) of certain kinds of light. From the information given in each question, determine the missing variables.

1. λ = 500. nm

2. f = 6.0×10^{14} Hz

3. E = 4.5×10^{-19} J

4. λ = 850. nm

5. f = 4.5×10^{13} Hz

6. E = 8.62×10^{-18} J

7. λ = 1250 nm

8. f = 8.22×10^{15} Hz

9. E = 1.22×10^{-20} J

10. λ = 355 nm

11. f = 3.362×10^{14} Hz

12. E = 3.604×10^{-17} J

II. The following questions concern electron transitions.

1. Calculate the total energy, in calories, required to ionize one mole of hydrogen atoms.

2. Find the values of E_n for the first three orbits of the hydrogen atom.

3. What energy is associated with a photon whose frequency is 4.3×10^{14} cycles per second?

4. What energy is emitted when an electron drops from the fourth to the second energy level in a hydrogen atom?

5. 10 Kcal/mole are emitted when an electron makes a particular transition from one orbit to another. What is the frequency of the photon that carries off this energy?

6. The energy absorbed by a particular atom during an electron transition from a lower to a higher level occurs as the absorption of red light of frequency 4.5×10^{14} cycles per second. What amount of energy is related to light of this frequency?

7. What is the total amount of energy absorbed by 1.0 mole of the substance in the case described in question 6?

8. An electron transition from a higher to a lower energy level in an atom results in a release of energy of 39.45 Kcal/mole. What is the frequency of the photon that carries off this energy?

9. Express the radius of the third orbit of the hydrogen atom, in terms of the radius of its lowest energy level, r.

10. Using Einstein's expression for the mass equivalence of energy, $E = mc^2$, express the wavelength of an electron in terms of its mass.

Electrochemistry

1. How much silver metal will be plated out in an electrolytic cell containing Ag^+ when 0.50 mol of electrons passes through the cell?

2. How much zinc metal will 2.5 mol of electrons plate out of a zinc chloride solution?

3. A current of 5.0 A is passed through a solution of aluminum chloride for 15 minutes. How much aluminum metal is plated out during this period of time?

4. How many amperes of current are needed to plate out 10.0 g of silver per hour from a solution of silver nitrate?

5. Determine the standard potential for each of the following cells and tell which half cell is the cathode in each case.

   a. Fe^{3+} (aq) | Fe^{2+} (aq); Ni^{2+} (aq) | Ni (s)

   b. Cu^{2+} (aq) | Cu (s); Ag^+ (aq) | Ag (s)

   c. Zn^{2+} (aq) | Zn (s); Ag^+ (aq) | Ag (s)

   d. Cu^{2+} (aq) | Cu (s); Cd^{2+} (aq) | Cd (s)

   e. Sn^{2+} (aq) | Sn (s); Br_2^0 (l) | Br^- (aq)

   f. Al^{3+} (aq) | Al (s); Cu^{2+} (aq) | Cu (s)

   g. Ni^{2+} (aq) | Ni (s); Cr^{3+} (aq) | Cr (s)

   h. Cd^{2+} (aq) | Cd (s); Co^{2+} (aq) | Co (s)

Appendix A

SOME USEFUL PHYSICAL CONSTANTS

Quantity	*Symbol*	*Numerical Value*
speed of light	c	2.9979246 x 10^8 m/s
elementary charge	e	1.6021892 x 10^{-19} C
Planck constant	h	6.626176 x 10^{-34} J/Hz
Avogadro number	N_A	6.022045 x 10^{23}/mol
rest mass of electron	m_e	9.109534 x 10^{-31} kg
rest mass of proton	m_p	1.6726485 x 10^{-27} kg
molar gas constant	R	8.31441 J/mol K

Appendix B

UNITS OF MEASURE

Base Units in the SI System

Quantity	*Unit*	*Symbol*
length	meter	m
mass	kilogram	kg
time	second	s
temperature	kelvin	K
electric current	ampere	A
luminous intensity	candela	cd
amount of substance	mole	mol

Derived Units in the SI System

Quantity	*Unit*	*Symbol*
force	newton	N
pressure	pascal	Pa
energy	joule	J
power	watt	W
charge	coulomb	C
voltage	volt	V

Appendix B *(continued)*

Other Common Units (not SI)

Quantity	*Unit*	*Symbol*
volume	liter	L
temperature	degree Celsius	°C

Metric Prefixes

Prefix	*Symbol*	*Value*
tera-	T	10^{12}
giga-	G	10^{9}
mega-	M	10^{6}
kilo-	k	10^{3}
hecto-	h	10^{2}
deka-	da	10^{1}
deci-	d	10^{-1}
centi-	c	10^{-2}
milli-	m	10^{-3}
micro-	μ	10^{-6}
nano-	n	10^{-9}
pico-	p	10^{-12}
femto-	f	10^{-15}
atto-	a	10^{-18}

Appendix C

SOME ENGLISH-METRIC CONVERSION FACTORS

Length
1 cm = 0.3937 in
1 ft = 0.3048 m

Mass
1 kg = 2.2046 lb
1 oz = 28.3495 g

Volume
1 L = 0.26417 U.S. gal
1 in^3 = 16.387 cm^3

Temperature
°C = 5/9 (°F – 32)
°F = 9/5 (°C) + 32

Appendix D

ATOMIC WEIGHTS AND ELECTRONIC CONFIGURATIONS OF THE ELEMENTS

Element	*Symbol*	*Atomic Number*	*Atomic Weight*	*Electronic Configuration*
actinium	Ac	89	(227)	Rn core $6d^{1}7s^{2}$
aluminum	Al	13	26.98154	Ne core $3s^{2}3p$
americium	Am	95	(243)	Rn core $5f^{7}7s^{2}$
antimony	Sb	51	121.75	Kr core $4d^{10}5s^{2}5p^{3}$
argon	Ar	18	39.948	$1s^{2}2s^{2}2p^{6}3s^{2}3p^{6}$
arsenic	As	33	74.9216	Ar core $3d^{10}4s^{2}4p^{3}$
astatine	At	85	(210)	Xe core $4f^{14}5d^{10}6s^{2}6p^{5}$
barium	Ba	56	137.33	Xe core $6s^{2}$
berkelium	Bk	97	(249)	Rn core $5f^{8}6d7s^{2}$
beryllium	Be	4	9.01218	He core $2s^{2}$
bismuth	Bi	83	208.9804	Xe core $4f^{14}5d^{10}6s^{2}6p^{3}$
boron	B	5	10.81	He core $2s^{2}2p$
bromine	Br	35	79.904	Ar core $3d^{10}4s^{2}4p^{5}$
cadmium	Cd	48	112.41	Kr core $4d^{10}5s^{2}$
calcium	Ca	20	40.08	Ar core $4s^{2}$
californium	Cf	98	(251)	Rn core $5f^{10}7s^{2}$
carbon	C	6	12.011	He core $2s^{2}2p^{2}$
cerium	Ce	58	140.12	Xe core $4f^{1}5d^{1}6s^{2}$
cesium	Cs	55	132.9054	Xe core 6s
chlorine	Cl	17	35.453	Ne core $3s^{2}3p^{5}$
chromium	Cr	24	51.996	Ar core $3d^{5}4s^{1}$
cobalt	Co	27	58.9332	Ar core $3d^{7}4s^{2}$
copper	Cu	29	63.546	Ar core $3d^{10}4s^{1}$
curium	Cm	96	(247)	Rn core $5f^{7}6d7s^{2}$
dysprosium	Dy	66	162.50	Xe core $4f^{10}6s^{2}$
einsteinium	Es	99	(254)	Rn core $5f^{11}7s^{2}$
erbium	Er	68	167.26	Xe core $4f^{12}6s^{2}$
europium	Eu	63	151.96	Xe core $4f^{7}6s^{2}$
fermium	Fm	100	(253)	Rn core $5f^{12}7s^{2}$
fluorine	F	9	18.998103	He core $2s^{2}2p^{5}$
francium	Fr	87	(223)	Rn core $7s^{1}$

Appendix D *(continued)*

Element	*Symbol*	*Atomic Number*	*Atomic Weight*	*Electronic Configuration*
gadolinium	Gd	64	157.25	Xe core $4f^7 5d^1 6s^2$
gallium	Ga	31	69.72	Ar core $3d^{10} 4s^2 4p$
germanium	Ge	32	72.59	Ar core $3d^{10} 4s^2 4p^2$
gold	Au	79	196.9665	Xe core $4f^{14} 5d^{10} 6s^1$
hafnium	Hf	72	178.49	Xe core $4f^{14} 5d^2 6s^2$
hahnium	Ha	105	(260)	Rn core $5f^{14} 6d^3 7s^2$
helium	He	2	4.00260	$1s^2$
holmium	Ho	67	164.9304	Xe core $4f^{11} 6s^2$
hydrogen	H	1	1.0079	1s
indium	In	49	114.82	Kr core $4d^{10} 5s^2 5p^1$
iodine	I	53	126.9045	Kr core $4d^{10} 5s^2 5p^5$
iridium	Ir	77	192.22	Xe core $4f^{14} 5d^7 6s^2$
iron	Fe	26	55.847	Ar core $3d^6 4s^2$
krypton	Kr	36	83.80	$ls^2 25^2 2p^6 35^2 3p^6 3d^{10} 45^2 4p^6$
kurchatovium	Ku	104	(247)	Rn core $5f^{14} 6d^2 7s^2$
lanthanum	La	57	138.9055	Xe core $5d^1 6s^2$
lawrencium	Lr	103	(257)	Rn core $5f^{14} 6d 7s^2$
lead	Pb	82	207.2	Xe core $4f^{14} 5d^{10} 6s^2 6p^2$
lithium	Li	3	6.941	He core 2s
lutetium	Lu	71	174.97	Xe core $4f^{14} 5d^1 6s^2$
magnesium	Mg	12	24.305	Ne core $3s^2$
manganese	Mn	25	54.94	Ar core $3d^5 4s^2$
mendelevium	Md	101	(256)	Rn core $5f^{13} 7s^2$
mercury	Hg	80	200.59	Xe core $4f^{14} 5d^{10} 6s^2$
molybdenum	Mo	42	95.94	Kr core $4d^5 5s^1$
neodymium	Nd	60	144.24	Xe core $4f^4 6s^2$
neon	Ne	10	20.179	$1s^2 2s^2 2p^6$
neptunium	Np	93	237.0482	Rn core $5f^4 6d 7s^2$
nickel	Ni	28	58.70	Ar core $3d^8 4s^2$
niobium	Nb	41	92.9064	Kr core $4d^4 5s^1$
nitrogen	N	7	14.0067	He core $2s^2 2p^3$
nobelium	No	102	(254)	Rn core $5f^{14} 7s^2$

Appendix D *(continued)*

Element	*Symbol*	*Atomic Number*	*Atomic Weight*	*Electronic Configuration*
osmium	Os	76	190.2	Xe core $4f^{14}5d^{6}6s^{2}$
oxygen	O	8	15.9994	He core $2s^{2}2p^{4}$
palladium	Pd	46	106.4	Kr core $4d^{10}$
phosphorus	P	15	30.97376	Ne core $3s^{2}3p^{3}$
platinum	Pt	78	195.09	Xe core $4f^{14}5d^{9}6s^{1}$
plutonium	Pu	94	(242)	Rn core $5f^{6}7s^{2}$
polonium	Po	84	(210)	Xe core $4f^{14}5d^{10}6s^{2}6p^{4}$
potassium	K	19	39.0983	Ar core 4s
praesodymium	Pr	59	140.9077	Xe core $4f^{3}6s^{2}$
promethium	Pm	61	(145)	Xe core $4f^{5}6s^{2}$
protactinium	Pa	91	231.0359	Rn core $5f^{2}6d7s^{2}$
radium	Ra	88	226.0254	Rn core $7s^{2}$
radon	Rn	86	(222)	$1s^{2}2s^{2}2p^{6}3s^{2}3p^{6}3d^{10}4s^{2}4p^{6}4d^{10}4f^{14}5s^{2}$ $5p^{6}5d^{10}6s^{2}6p^{6}$
rhenium	Re	75	186.207	Xe core $4f^{14}5d^{5}6s^{2}$
rhodium	Rh	45	102.9055	Kr core $4d^{8}5s^{1}$
rubidium	Rb	37	85.4678	Kr core 5s
ruthenium	Ru	44	101.07	Kr core $4d^{7}5s^{1}$
samarium	Sm	62	150.4	Xe core $4f^{6}6s^{2}$
scandium	Sc	21	44.9559	Ar core $3d^{1}4s^{2}$
selenium	Se	34	78.96	Ar core $3d^{10}4s^{2}4p^{4}$
silicon	Si	14	28.0855	Ne core $3s^{2}3p^{2}$
silver	Ag	47	107.868	Kr core $4d^{10}5s^{1}$
sodium	Na	11	22.98977	Ne core 3s
strontium	Sr	38	87.62	Kr core $5s^{2}$
sulfur	S	16	32.06	Ne core $3s^{2}3p^{4}$
tantalum	Ta	73	180.9479	Xe core $4f^{14}5d^{3}6s^{2}$
technetium	Tc	43	98.9062	Kr core $4d^{5}5s^{2}$
tellurium	Te	52	127.60	Kr core $4d^{10}5s^{2}5p^{4}$
terbium	Tb	65	158.9254	Xe core $4f^{9}6s^{2}$
thallium	Tl	81	204.37	Xe core $4f^{14}5d^{10}6s^{2}6p^{1}$
thorium	Th	90	232.0381	Rn core $6d^{2}7s^{2}$

Appendix D *(continued)*

Element	*Symbol*	*Atomic Number*	*Atomic Weight*	*Electronic Configuration*
thulium	Tm	69	168.9342	Xe core $4f^{13}6s^2$
tin	Sn	50	118.69	Kr core $4d^{10}5s^25p^2$
titanium	Ti	22	47.90	Ar core $3d^24s^2$
tungsten	W	74	183.85	Xe core $4f^{14}5d^46s^2$
uranium	U	92	238.029	Rn core $5f^36d7s^2$
vanadium	V	23	50.9444	Ar core $3d^34s^2$
xenon	Xe	54	131.30	$1s^22s^22p^63s^23p^63d^{10}4s^24p^64d^{10}5s^25p^6$
ytterbium	Yb	70	173.04	Xe core $4f^{14}6s^2$
yttrium	Y	39	88.9059	Kr core $4d^15s^2$
zinc	Zn	30	65.38	Ar core $3d^{10}4s^2$
zirconium	Zr	40	91.22	Kr core $4d^25s^2$
[not assigned]		106	(263)	Rn core $5f^{14}6d^47s^2$

Atomic weights are based on carbon 12. Values in parentheses are the mass numbers of the most stable or best known isotopes of the elements.

Appendix E

DENSITY OF SOME COMMON MATERIALS

Substance	*Density*
air	1.293 g/L
alcohol (ethyl)	0.79 g/cm^3
aluminum	2.70 g/cm^3
brass	8.4 – 8.7 g/cm^3
carbon (graphite)	2.25 g/cm^3
carbon dioxide	1.997 g/L

Appendix E *(continued)*

Substance	*Density*
copper	8.89 g/cm^3
ether	0.74 g/cm^3
gasoline	0.68 g/cm^3
glass	2.4 – 2.8 g/cm^3
gold	19.3 g/cm^3
hydrogen	0.090 g/L
ice	0.917 g/cm^3
iron (wrought)	7.85 g/cm^3
lead	11.3 g/cm^3
mercury	13.6 g/cm^3
nitrogen	1.25 g/L
oxygen	1.43 g/L
silver	10.5 g/cm^3
steel	7.80 g/cm^3
water (20° C)	0.998 g/cm^3
water (4° C)	1.000 g/cm^3
zinc	7.1 g/cm^3

Appendix F

ELECTRONEGATIVITIES OF THE ELEMENTS

H 2.1																
Li 1.0	Be 1.5											B 2.0	C 2.5	N 3.1	O 3.5	F 4.1
Na 1.0	Mg 1.3											Al 1.5	Si 1.8	P 2.1	S 2.4	Cl 2.9
K 0.9	Ca 1.1	Sc 1.2	Ti 1.3	V 1.5	Cr 1.6	Mn 1.6	Fe 1.7	Co 1.7	Ni 1.8	Cu 1.8	Zn 1.7	Ga 1.8	Ge 2.0	As 2.2	Se 2.5	Br 2.8
Rb 0.9	Sr 1.0	Y 1.1	Zr 1.2	Nb 1.3	Mo 1.3	Tc 1.4	Ru 1.4	Rh 1.5	Pd 1.4	Ag 1.4	Cd 1.5	In 1.5	Sn 1.7	Sb 1.8	Te 2.0	I 2.2
Cs 0.9	Ba 0.9	La 1.1	Hf 1.2	Ta 1.4	W 1.4	Re 1.5	Os 1.5	Ir 1.6	Pt 1.5	Au 1.4	Hg 1.5	Tl 1.5	Pb 1.6	Bi 1.7	Po 1.8	At 2.0
Fr 0.9	Ra 0.9	Ac 1.0														

Lanthanides: 1.0–1.2
Actinides: 1.0–1.2

For practice problems, assume that differences in electronegativities of less than 0.4 between two bonding atoms result in a non-polar covalent bond, differences between 0.4 and 1.7 result in a polar covalent bond, and differences greater than 1.7 result in an ionic bond.

Appendix G

HEATS OF FORMATION

Compound	*Heat of formation* (in kilocalories per mole)	*Compound*	*Heat of formation* (in kilocalories per mole)
$AlCl_3$	166.2	P_2O_5	360.0
$NH_3(g)$	11.0	KBr	93.7
NH_4Cl	75.4	KCl	104.2
$BaCl_2$	205.6	$KClO_3$	93.5
BaO	133.4	KI	78.3
$CaCO_3$	288.4	KNO_3	117.8
$CaCl_2$	190.0	KOH	101.8
CaO	151.9	AgCl	30.4
$CH_4(g)$	17.9	$AgNO_3$	29.4
$CO_2(g)$	94.0	NaBr	86.0
CO(g)	26.4	NaCl	98.2
$CCl_4(l)$	33.2	NaF	136.0
$CuCl_2$	52.3	$SO_2(g)$	71.0
CuO	37.1	$SO_3(l)$	103.0
Cu_2O	39.8	$SnCl_2$	83.6
$CuSO_4$	184.0	$H_2O(l)$	68.3
HBr(g)	8.7	$H_2O_2(l)$	44.8
HCl(g)	22.1	$H_2S(g)$	4.8
HF(g)	64.2	$H_2SO_4(l)$	913.9
HI(g)	-6.2	$FeCl_3$	96.8
$HNO_3(l)$	41.4	FeS	22.7
PbO	52.1	$SnCl_4(l)$	130.3
$MgCl_2$	153.4	$ZnCl_2$	99.4
HgO	21.7	$Zn(NO_3)_2$	115.1
NO(g)	-21.6	ZnO	83.2
$N_2O(g)$	19.5	$Zn(OH)_2$	153.5
NO_2	-8.1	ZnS	48.5

Appendix H

SPECIFIC HEAT, HEAT OF FUSION, AND HEAT OF VAPORIZATION OF SOME SELECTED SUBSTANCES

Substance	*Specific Heat* (cal/g · °C)	*Heat of Fusion* (cal/g)	*Heat of Vaporization* (cal/g)
alcohol (ethyl)	0.60	26	210
aluminum	0.215	94.5	2570
benzene	0.34	30	131
chloroform	0.232	19	63
copper	0.092	49.0	1270
ether (ethyl)	0.56	24	88
ice	0.50	79.8	540
iron	0.11	63.7	1780
lead	0.031	5.9	226
magnesium	0.243	88.9	1450
mercury	0.033	2.7	68
steam	0.482	79.8	540
water	1.0000	79.8	540

Appendix I

VAPOR PRESSURE OF WATER (in millimeters of mercury)

temperature (°C)	*pressure* (mmHg)	*temperature* (°C)	*pressure* (mmHg)	*temperature* (°C)	*pressure* (mmHg)
1	4.9	5	6.5	9	8.6
2	5.3	6	7.0	10	9.2
3	5.7	7	7.5	11	9.8
4	6.1	8	8.0	12	10.5

Appendix I *(continued)*

temperature (°C)	*pressure* (mmHg)	*temperature* (°C)	*pressure* (mmHg)	*temperature* (°C)	*pressure* (mmHg)
13	11.2	29	30.0	45	71.9
14	12.0	30	31.8	46	75.6
15	12.8	31	33.7	47	79.6
16	13.6	32	35.7	48	83.7
17	14.5	33	37.7	49	88.0
18	15.5	34	39.9	50	92.5
19	16.5	35	42.2	55	118.0
20	17.5	36	44.6	60	149.4
21	18.6	37	47.1	65	187.5
22	19.8	38	49.7	70	233.7
23	21.1	39	52.4	75	289.1
24	22.4	40	55.3	80	355.1
25	23.8	41	58.3	85	433.6
26	25.2	42	61.5	90	525.8
27	26.7	43	64.8	95	633.9
28	28.3	44	68.3	100	760.0

Appendix J

BOILING POINT ELEVATION AND FREEZING POINT DEPRESSION CONSTANTS

Substance	*Normal Boiling Point* (°C)	*Boiling Point Elevation* (°C)	*Normal Freezing Point* (°C)	*Freezing Point Depression* (°C)
acetic acid	118.1	2.53	16.6	3.90
benzene	80.1	2.53	5.5	5.12
camphor	207.4	5.61	179.5	37.7

Appendix J *(continued)*

Substance	*Normal Boiling Point* (°C)	*Boiling Point Elevation* (°C)	*Normal Freezing Point* (°C)	*Freezing Point Depression* (°C)
carbon tetrachloride	76.8	4.48	−23.0	29.8
chloroform	61.2	3.62	−63.5	4.68
cyclohexane	80.7	2.75	6.5	6.54
1,2-dibromoethane	131.7	6.61	10	12.5
ethyl alcohol	78.4	1.16	−114.6	1.99
naphthalene	218.0	5.80	80.2	6.94
water	100.0	0.52	0.0	1.86

Appendix K

ACTIVITY SERIES OF THE ELEMENTS

Metals		*Non-metals*
lithium	cobalt	fluorine
rubidium	nickel	chlorine
potassium	tin	bromine
sodium	lead	iodine
strontium	HYDROGEN	sulfur
barium	antimony	
calcium	bismuth	
magnesium	arsenic	
aluminum	copper	
manganese	mercury	
zinc	silver	
chromium	platinum	
iron	gold	
cadmium		

Appendix L

TABLE OF SOLUBILITIES

Initial note: All common compounds containing sodium or potassium or the ammonium, chlorate, or nitrate radical are soluble in water and are not listed in the following table.

S = soluble in water

P = partially soluble in water

I = insoluble in water and in dilute acids

A = insoluble in water, soluble in dilute acids

a = partially soluble in dilute acids; insoluble in water

X = does not exist or decomposes in water

	acetate	bromide	carbonate	chloride	chromate	hydroxide	iodide	oxide	phosphate	silicate	sulfate	sulfide
aluminum	S	S	X	S	X	A	S	a	A	I	S	X
barium	S	S	P	S	A	S	S	S	A	S	a	X
calcium	S	S	P	S	S	S	S	P	P	P	P	P
cupric	S	S	X	S	X	A	X	A	A	A	S	A
ferrous	S	S	P	S	X	A	S	A	A	X	S	A
ferric	S	S	X	S	A	A	S	A	P	X	P	X
lead	S	S	A	S	A	P	S	P	A	A	P	A
magnesium	S	S	P	S	S	A	S	A	P	A	S	X
manganese	S	S	P	S	X	A	S	A	P	I	S	A
mercurous	P	A	A	a	P	X	A	A	A	X	P	I
mercuric	S	S	X	S	P	A	P	P	A	X	X	I
silver	P	a	A	a	P	X	I	P	A	X	P	A
stannous	X	S	X	S	A	A	S	A	A	X	S	A
stannic	S	S	X	X	S	P	X	A	X	X	S	A
strontium	S	S	P	S	P	S	S	S	A	A	P	S
zinc	S	S	P	S	P	A	S	P	A	A	S	A

Appendix M

HALF LIVES OF SOME COMMON RADIOACTIVE ISOTOPES

Isotope	*Half Life*
^{3}H	12.3 y
^{14}C	5730 y
^{15}O	124 s
^{24}Na	15.0 h
^{32}P	14.3 d
^{40}K	1.28×10^{9} y
^{51}Cr	27.8 d
^{55}Fe	2.6 y
^{60}Co	5.26 y
^{85}Sr	70 m
^{99m}Tc	6.0 h
^{131}I	8.1 d
^{198}Au	2.7 d
^{226}Ra	1600 y
^{234}Th	24 d
^{235}U	7.1×10^{8} y
^{238}U	4.5×10^{9} y
^{239}Np	2.35 d
^{239}Pu	24,400 y

Appendix N

LOGARITHMS OF NUMBERS FROM 1.0 to 9.9

Number	.0	.1	.2	.3	.4	.5	.6	.7	.8	.9
1	.00	.04	.08	.11	.15	.18	.20	.23	.26	.28
2	.30	.32	.34	.36	.38	.40	.42	.43	.45	.46
3	.48	.49	.51	.52	.53	.54	.56	.57	.58	.59
4	.60	.61	.62	.63	.64	.65	.66	.67	.68	.69
5	.70	.71	.72	.72	.73	.74	.75	.76	.76	.77
6	.78	.79	.79	.80	.81	.81	.82	.83	.83	.84
7	.85	.85	.86	.86	.87	.88	.88	.89	.89	.90
8	.90	.91	.91	.92	.92	.93	.93	.94	.94	.95
9	.95	.96	.96	.97	.97	.98	.98	.99	.99	1.00

Appendix O

SOME STANDARD REDUCTION POTENTIALS
(at 25° C and 1 mol conc)

Electrode	*Half Reaction*	E^o
$Li^+ \vert Li$	$Li^+ + e^- \rightarrow Li$	-3.05
$K^+ \vert K$	$K^+ + e^- \rightarrow K$	-2.93
$Ca^{2+} \vert Ca$	$Ca^{2+} + 2\,e^- \rightarrow Ca$	-2.87
$Na^+ \vert Na$	$Na^+ + e^- \rightarrow Na$	-2.71
$Mg^{2+} \vert Mg$	$Mg^{2+} + 2\,e^- \rightarrow Mg$	-2.37
$Al^{3+} \vert Al$	$Al^{3+} + 3\,e^- \rightarrow Al$	-1.66
$Zn^{2+} \vert Zn$	$Zn^{2+} + 2\,e^- \rightarrow Zn$	-0.76
$Cr^{3+} \vert Cr$	$Cr^{3+} + 3e^- \rightarrow Cr$	-0.74
$Fe^{2+} \vert Fe$	$Fe^{2+} + 2\,e^- \rightarrow Fe$	-0.44
$Cd^{2+} \vert Cd$	$Cd^{2+} + 2\,e^- \rightarrow Cd$	-0.40
$Co^{2+} \vert Co$	$Co^{2+} + 2\,e^- \rightarrow Co$	-0.28
$Ni^{2+} \vert Ni$	$Ni^{2+} + 2\,e^- \rightarrow Ni$	-0.25
$Sn^{2+} \vert Sn$	$Sn^{2+} + 2\,e^- \rightarrow Sn$	-0.14
$Pb^{2+} \vert Pb$	$Pb^{2+} + 2\,e^- \rightarrow Pb$	-0.13
$Fe^{3+} \vert Fe$	$Fe^{3+} + 2\,e^- \rightarrow Fe$	-0.036
$H^+ \vert H_2$	$2H^+ + 2\,e^- \rightarrow H_2$	-0.00
$Cu^{2+} \vert Cu$	$Cu^{2+} + 2\,e^- \rightarrow Cu$	+0.34
$Cu^+ \vert Cu$	$Cu^+ + e^- \rightarrow Cu$	+0.52
$Fe^{3+} \vert Fe^{2+}$	$Fe^{3+} + e^- \rightarrow Fe^{3+}$	+0.77
$Hg_2^{2+} \vert Hg$	$Hg_2^{2+} + 2\,e^- \rightarrow 2\,Hg$	+0.34
$Ag^+ \vert Ag$	$Ag^+ + e^- \rightarrow Ag$	+0.80
$Hg_2^{2+} \vert Hg$	$Hg_2^{2+} + 2\,e^- \rightarrow Hg$	+0.85
$Br_2 \vert Br^-$	$Br_2 + 2\,e^- \rightarrow Br^-$	+1.07
$Cl_2 \vert Cl^-$	$Cl_2 + 2\,e^- \rightarrow Cl^-$	+1.36
$F_2 \vert F^-$	$F_2 + 2\,e^- \rightarrow F^-$	+2.87

Answers

NOTE: Student answers may differ slightly from those given here depending on the atomic weight table used and the method of rounding suggested by the teacher.

Exponential Notation: pp. 1-3

Group I.

1. 1×10^{4}
2. 1×10^{-4}
3. 1×10^{10}
4. 5×10^{4}
5. 2×10^{9}
6. 4×10^{-7}
7. 3×10^{-4}
8. 7.9×10^{5}
9. 2.6×10^{13}
10. 4.5×10^{-8}
11. 4.8×10^{7}
12. 1.3×10^{-18}
13. 1.75×10^{-2}
14. 4.62×10^{-5}
15. 3×10^{6}
16. 9.2×10^{6}
17. 3.71×10^{2}
18. 9.00×10^{-3}
19. 6.2×10^{-1}
20. 1.97×10^{-4}
21. 3.285×10^{5}
22. 7.645×10^{4}
23. 9.410×10^{-1}
24. 3.005×10^{3}
25. 7.05×10^{-4}
26. 8×10^{10}
27. 6.24×10^{3}
28. 1.75×10^{7}
29. 5.302×10^{-2}
30. 9.15×10^{-12}
31. 2.8×10^{1}
32. 7.480×10^{0}
33. 2.805×10^{8}
34. 1.342×10^{2}
35. 8.9×10^{-5}

Group II.

1. 100,000
2. 0.000,000,000,001
3. 400
4. 0.000,005
5. 0.032
6. 0.795
7. 685,400,000,000,000
8. 1430
9. 0.0009065
10. 4300
11. 442,000,000
12. 0.00308
13. 16.9
14. 663,000
15. 0.00000400

*Group III.**

1. 24
2. 1×10^{-5}
3. 20
4. 4.58×10^{3}
5. 1.35×10^{10}
6. 3×10^{-2}
7. 8×10^{-6}
8. 8×10^{-2}
9. 7.9×10^{9}
10. 1.47×10^{5}
11. 5×10^{-3}
12. 48
13. 8×10^{-7}
14. 3×10^{3}
15. 4×10^{-2}
16. 8.2×10^{3}
17. 2×10^{-3}
18. 2×10^{-4}

**In addition to those given here equivalent correct answers are possible.*

(continued)

19. 1.8×10^{-5}
20. 9×10^{-10}
21. 8×10^{3}
22. 5×10^{11}
23. 3.839×10^{4}
24. .24
25. 2×10^{7}
26. 5.2×10^{-2}
27. 4.48×10^{3}
28. 2.4×10^{-8}
29. 2×10^{-4}
30. 1.12×10^{7}
31. 6.1×10^{-2}
32. 8×10^{-10}
33. 4×10^{6}
34. 4.883×10^{-2}
35. 64
36. 2.8×10^{10}
37. 3.2
38. .01
39. 2×10^{-8}
40. 5×10^{-7}
41. 2×10^{4}
42. 4.5×10^{6}
43. 5×10^{-5}
44. 8×10^{-9}
45. 3×10^{4}
46. 2×10^{5}
47. 7×10^{-9}
48. 1.33×10^{14}
49. 5×10^{12}
50. 6.66×10^{-12}

Significant Figures: pp. 4–8

Group I.

1. 4
2. 5
3. 3
4. 4
5. 3
6. 4
7. 5
8. 3
9. 3
10. 3
11. 2, 3, or 4
12. 5
13. 3
14. 3
15. 7
16. 5
17. 4
18. 4
19. 3
20. 4

Group II.

1. **20. cm**
2. **0.29 cm**
3. **14.383 g**
4. **173.6 g**
5. **506.7 cm**
6. **246.62 cm**
7. **0.2704 g**
8. **3.89×10^{-4} cm**
9. **270.6 mL**
10. **10.8×10^{2} g**

Group III.

1. **17.74 cm**
2. **245 g**
3. **116.7 mL**
4. **22.6 g**
5. **10.914 mL**

Group IV.

1. 11.6 cm^2
2. 110 cm^2
3. 3.7 m^2
4. 36.6 mm^2
5. 2560 dm^2
6. 20 cm^2
7. 20 cm^2
8. 25 cm^2
9. $10. \times 10^{5}$ m^2 1.0×10^{6}
10. 11×10^{-7} cm^2
11. 27 cm^2
12. 600. m^2
13. 850 km^2
14. 46×10^{-14} m^2
15. 4.21×10^{7} m^2

Group V.

1. 1.914 cm
2. 18.82 m
3. 570. km
4. 7.1 mm
5. 0.4891 cm
6. 2.029 m
7. 0.223 m
8. 10.6 km
9. 1.036×10^2 mm
10. 1.3×10^{-5} mm

Group VI.

1. 0.064 mL
2. 137 mL
3. 19.9 g
4. 55.479 g
5. 7.329×10^{16} cm^3

Group VII.

1. 0.0109 g/cm^3; -7.37%
2. -0.02 g; -0.51%
3. 1.3°C; 0.75%
4. -3 lb; -1.69%
5. -0.0964 g; -90.77%
6. 0.5 mL; 0.5%
7. -0.69 dynes/cm; -0.96%
8. -0.0013 g; -0.0232%
9. -0.0009 N; -0.6598%
10. +9.3% error in first case; -9.3% error in the second. The errors have the same magnitude, but different directions.
11. 1.5112 g/cm^3; 1.3672 g/cm^3
12. 86.670 g; 82.442 g
13. Minimum value: 865.4 cm
    Maximum value: 866.2 cm
14. 0.03 g
15. 1269
16. 8
17. 50.0 ± 2.25 cm^2
18. $D = 0.1823 \pm 0.0006$ g/cm^3
19. a. 18.514 g b. 0.002 g
20. Heat absorbed = $23{,}220 \pm 193$ cal

Dimensional Analysis: p. 9

1. 0.14 m
2. 31,000 mg
3. 0.1165 km
4. 0.002859 km
5. 639.4 cm
6. 0.84 cg
7. 0.147 km
8. 10. lb (10.4 lb)
9. 3924 g
10. 40.7 mi
11. 719 cm
12. 0.273 d
13. 14.4 liq qt
14. 12.8 mi/hr
15. 5.8 cm/s
16. 0.969 m/s
17. 918 lb/ft^3
18. 2.23×10^{-3} ft^3/d
19. 8.05×10^5 kg/L
20. 1670 g/cm^2

Metric System: pp. 10–17

Group I.

1. 2,100,000
2. 16530
3. 2.38
4. 10.6
5. 420
6. 3.01×10^{-5}
7. 410.5
8. 90,000
9. 13520
10. 4.6×10^{-1}
11. 96,000
12. 240,000

Group II.

1. 93.8
2. 1930
3. 22.8
4. 40,500
5. 24320
6. 2.8
7. 85
8. 3.1×10^4
9. 6.3×10^3
10. 370,000
11. 8.012×10^{10}
12. 42,000

Group III.

1. 7.3456
2. 0.369
3. 0.41
4. 15.2
5. 1.24
6. 1428.1
7. 8950
8. 2.3
9. 21,000
10. .00238

Group IV.

1. 0.415
2. 1760
3. 978.5
4. 9900
5. 337
6. 0.285
7. 0.753
8. 0.014587
9. 2.81
10. 1000 (1043)
11. 0.423
12. 0.0134

Group V.

1. 2.450
2. 14.72
3. 0.0899
4. 10.8
5. 0.023
6. 2.83×10^{-4}
7. 0.654
8. 2.4×10^2
9. 1.47
10. 0.6

Group VI.

1. 31
2. .2985
3. 0.000159
4. 110
5. 12.9
6. 0.888
7. 0.0014
8. 1.1×10^{-4}
9. 0.086
10. 9.3

Group VII.

1. 0.836
2. 3.1×10^{-4}
3. 0.0116
4. 37.7
5. 1.405×10^{-3}
6. 4.2×10^{-8}
7. 69
8. 0.0164
9. 1100
10. 0.0262

Group VIII.

1. 0.182
2. 3.2
3. 4.0
4. 895
5. 0.1354
6. 0.750
7. 0.0229
8. 0.0432
9. 0.158
10. 0.028
11. 60 (57)
12. 0.250

Group IX.

1. 14200
2. 2590.1
3. 9.23×10^{-3}
4. 6810
5. 232
6. 148
7. 416
8. 4380
9. 243
10. 1.079×10^{-12}

Group X.

1. 15.1
2. 0.268
3. 74.5
4. 0.0586
5. 3.2
6. 408.8
7. 63.7
8. 0.135
9. 9.51×10^{-3}
10. 11.8

Group XI.

1. 0.016
2. 854
3. 4.32×10^{-5}
4. 4.8×10^{-5}
5. 1830
6. 0.125
7. 234,500,000
8. 1420
9. 319
10. 7680
11. 6.0×10^{-3}
12. 927

Group XII.

1. 36.7
2. 12.4
3. 290
4. 183
5. 2.0×10^{3}
6. 360
7. 28
8. 8590
9. 85
10. 287
11. 7.41×10^{-3}
12. 1.047×10^{-5}

Group XIII.

1. 145
2. 0.0515
3. 570
4. 1.44
5. 3.21×10^{6}
6. 1.4×10^{-5}
7. 26.9
8. 6.7×10^{-5}
9. 6.28×10^{-4}
10. 10.7

Group XIV.

1. 1600
2. 1.0×10^{-3}
3. 0.785
4. 3.90
5. 0.0254
6. 0.0344
7. 468
8. 0.21
9. 6.808×10^{-7}
10. 99

Group XV.

1. 2.3896×10^{-4}
2. 0.01427
3. 4.12
4. 0.166
5. 11
6. 37.1×10^{4}
7. 0.0023
8. 0.00763
9. 2.3×10^{-7}
10. 0.0435

Group XVI.

1. 9.65
2. 17.2
3. 16.3
4. 2.80
5. 25
6. 7.3795
7. 300
8. 149
9. 122
10. 9.598×10^{-6}

Group XVII.

1. 18.6
2. 0.0919
3. 2.316×10^{4}
4. 1.32
5. 16.6
6. 0.33
7. 10.31
8. 2.04×10^{3}
9. .221
10. 3.97

Group XVIII.

1. 8.1
2. 4.04×10^{-3}
3. 16.8
4. 1.90×10^{-5}
5. 0.0179
6. 0.413
7. 0.2348
8. 46.3
9. .032
10. .09966

Group XIX.

1. 1000
2. 3.29×10^{6}
3. 5800
4. 8.9×10^{4}
5. 1.1075
6. 1.016×10^{5}
7. 0.4812
8. 6.9×10^{-9}
9. 4.28×10^{-2}
10. 1.29×10^{5}

Group XX.

1. 6.34×10^{8}
2. 640
3. 4.017×10^{8}
4. 1.080×10^{7}
5. 7.5×10^{8}
6. 3.0×10^{12}
7. 2.54×10^{8}
8. 9.0×10^{4}
9. 9.7×10^{9}
10. 1.111×10^{6}

Group XXI.

1. 4.5×10^{12} pg
2. 8.2×10^{6} ng
3. 6.5×10^{7} pg
4. 3.17×10^{6} ng
5. 2.9×10^{8} pg
6. 1.5×10^{3} ng
7. 1.23×10^{5} pg
8. 8.85 ng
9. 3.6 pg
10. 4.28×10^{2} ng
11. 2.86×10^{4} pg
12. 0.153 ng

Group XXII.

1. 340 g
2. 4.2 cm
3. 6.300 cm
4. 92 mL
5. 600 mL
6. 437.4 yd
7. 48.42 gal
8. 1.3×10^{-6} cm^3
9. 41 s
10. 0.071 cm
11. 1022 cm^3
12. 22 cm
13. 93 g
14. 2.0 min
15. 11 bottles

Energy: pp. 18–21

Group I.

1. 0° C
2. 14° C
3. −15° C
4. 59.78° C
5. −41.3° C
6. −22° C
7. 0° C
8. 40° C
9. 57.2° C
10. 133.1° C
11. −138.5° C
12. −224.3° C

Group II.

1. 212° F
2. 32° F
3. 79° F
4. 347.7° F
5. −40.0° F
6. −247.5° F
7. 95.0° F
8. 190° F
9. 53.4° F
10. −106.° F
11. 289.9° F
12. −299° F

Group III.

1. 283 K
2. 351 K
3. 308.6 K
4. 539.3 K
5. 432.5 K
6. 208.7 K
7. 264.7 K
8. 314.3 K
9. 290.5 K
10. 374.4 K
11. 234.1 K
12. 109.5 K

Group IV.

1. 800. cal
2. 1130 cal
3. 1060 cal
4. 10,100 cal
5. 7980. cal
6. 21,600 cal
7. 129 cal
8. 3960. cal
9. 222 cal
10. 5020 cal
11. 18,000 cal
12. 282 cal
13. 9129 cal
14. 12,200 cal
15. 299,100 cal
16. 4.7 cal
17. 7990 cal
18. 19,270 cal
19. 7250 cal
20. 26,900 cal

Group V.

1. 332,000 cal/mol
2. Reactions b. and c.
3. 10,080 cal
4. −22.25 cal/°K
5. $\Delta H^\circ = 15{,}750$ cal
6. $\Delta H^\circ_{25} = -67.4$ Kcal (exothermic)
7. 68,300 Kcal of heat is given off
8. $\Delta H = -67.6$ Kcal
9. $\Delta H = -341$ Kcal
10. (a) 22.1 J/K mol; (b) 109 J/K mol
11. 28.6 kJ
12. 91.4 kJ

Atomic Structure: pp. 22–27

Group I.

In the following answers, the order given is number of protons, number of neutrons, number of electrons, arrangement of electrons.

1. 8, 8, 8, 2-6
2. 3, 4, 3, 2-1
3. 20, 20, 20, 2-8-8-2
4. 16, 16, 16, 2-8-6
5. 18, 22, 18, 2-8-8
6. 6, 6, 6, 2-4
7. 19, 20, 19, 2-8-8-1
8. 2, 2, 2, 2
9. 13, 14, 13, 2-8-3
10. 1, 0, 1, 1
11. 4, 5, 4, 2-2
12. 9, 10, 9, 2-7
13. 7, 7, 7, 2-5
14. 33, 42, 33, 2-8-18-5
15. 83, 126, 83, 2-8-18-32-18-5
16. 79, 118, 79, 2-8-18-32-18-1
17. 44, 57, 44, 2-8-18-15-1
18. 78, 117, 78, 2-8-18-32-17-1
19. 27, 32, 27, 2-8-15-2
20. 21, 24, 21, 2-8-9-2

Group II.

Refer to Appendix D.

Group III.

In the following answers, the quantum numbers are given in the order n, l, m, s. Where a choice of possible answers is available, the answers are placed within parentheses.

1. 1, 0, 0, ± ½; 2, 0, 0, ± ½; 2, 1, 0, + ½ or − ½
2. 1, 0, 0, ± ½; 2, 0, 0, ± ½; 2, 1, 0, ± ½; 3 of the following (2, 1, ± 1 ± ½)
3. 1, 0, 0, ± ½; 2, 0, 0, ± ½; 2, 1, 0, ± ½; 2, 1, ± 1, ± ½; 3, 0, 0, + ½ or − ½
4. 1, 0, 0, ± ½; 2, 0, 0, ± ½; 2, 1, 0, ± ½; 2, 1, ± 1, ± ½; 3, 0, 0, ± ½; 3, 1, 0, ± ½; 3, 1, ± 1, ± ½
5. 1, 0, 0, ± ½; 2, 0, 0, ± ½; 2, 1, 0, ± ½; 2 of the following (2, 1, ± 1, ± ½)
6. 1, 0, 0, ± ½; 2, 0, 0, ± ½
7. 1, 0, 0, ± ½; 2, 0, 0, ± ½; 2, 1, 0, ± ½; 2, 1, ± 1, ± ½; 3, 0, 0, ± ½; 3, 1, 0, ± ½; 3, 1, ± 1, ± ½; 4, 0, 0, ± ½ or −½
8. 1, 0, 0, ± ½ or −½
9. 1, 0, 0, ± ½; 2, 0, 0, ± ½; 2, 1, 0, ± ½; 2, 1, ± 1, ± ½; 3, 0, 0, ± ½
10. 1, 0, 0, ± ½; 2, 0, 0, ± ½
11. 1, 0, 0, ± ½; 2, 0, 0, + ½ or −½
12. 1, 0, 0, ± ½; 2, 0, 0, ± ½; 2, 1, 0, ± ½

Group IV.

In the following answers, p stands for protons and n for neutrons:

1. 1 p, 0 n; 1 p, 1 n
2. 3 p, 3 n; 3 p, 4 n
3. 5 p, 5 n; 5 p, 6 n
4. 17 p, 18 n; 17 p, 20 n
5. 18 p, 17 n; 18 p, 20 n; 18 p, 22 n

(continued)

6. 32 p, 38 n; 32 p, 40 n; 32 p, 41 n; 32 p, 42 n; 32 p, 44 n
7. 92 p, 142 n; 92 p, 146 n
8. 52 p, 70 n; 52 p, 72 n; 52 p, 74 n; 52 p, 76 n
9. 54 p, 75 n; 54 p, 76 n; 54 p, 77 n; 54 p, 78 n; 54 p, 80 n; 54 p, 82 n
10. 63 p, 88 n; 63 p, 90 n

Group V.

(Please note that isotopic compositions have been altered slightly so as to give atomic masses somewhat different from those found elsewhere.)

1. 1.00015
2. 6.9258
3. 10.8022
4. 35.4894
5. 39.9819
6. 72.7156
7. 237.972
8. 127.785
9. 131.475
10. 151.522

Group VI.

1.
   a. 8
   b. 5
   c. 1
   d. 7
   e. 2
   f. 4
   g. 3
   h. 6

2.
   a. [Xe] $4f^{14}5d^{10}6s^26p^3$
   b. [Xe] $4f^{14}5d^{10}6s^2$
   c. [Xe]
   d. [Xe] $6s^1$
   e. [Kr] $5s^1$
   f. [Kr]
   g. [Ar] $3d^54s^2$
   h. [Ar]

3.
   a. N
   b. Be
   c. P
   d. Mn
   e. K
   f. Zr
   g. Pm
   h. Se

4.
   a. [Ar] $3d^{10}4s^1$; [Ar] $3d^{10}$; [Ar] $3d^9$
   b. [Ne] $3s^23p^1$; [Ne]
   c. [Ne] $3s^23p^5$; [Ne] $3s^23p^6$
   d. [He] $2s^22p^4$; [He] $2s^22p^6$; [He] $2s^22p^5$
   e. [Ne] $3s^23p^4$; [Ne] $3s^23p^2$; [Ne] $3s^2$; [Ne]; [Ne] $3s^23p^6$
   f. [Ne] $3s^23p^3$; [Ne] ; [Ne] $3s^2$; [Ne] $3s^23p^6$

5.
   a. potassium:

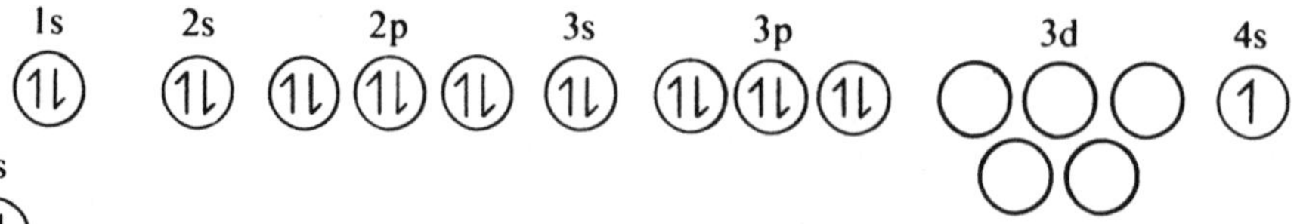

   b. helium:

   c. beryllium ion:

(continued)

d. nitrogen: 1s (↑↓) 2s (↑↓) 2p (↑)(↑)(↑)

e. fluoride ion: 1s (↑↓) 2s (↑↓) 2p (↑↓)(↑↓)(↑)

f. sulfur: 1s (↑↓) 2s (↑↓) 2p (↑↓)(↑↓)(↑↓) 3s (↑↓) (↑↓)(↑)(↑)

g. silicon: 1s (↑↓) 2s (↑↓) 2p (↑↓)(↑↓)(↑↓) 3s (↑↓) 3p (↑)(↑)( )

h. neon: 1s (↑↓) 2s (↑↓) 2p (↑↓)(↑↓)(↑↓)

6.

a. 

b. 

c. 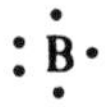

d. H·

e. 

f. 

g. Na·

h. K^{+}

i. 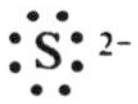

j. Mg^{2+}

k. B^{3+}

l. 

7.

a. oxygen: 2s ⊗ 2p ⊗⊘⊘

b. boron: 2s ⊗ 2p ⊗○○

c. aluminum: 3s ⊗ 3p ⊘○○

d. calcium: 4s ⊗

e. Na^{+}: 2s ⊗ 2p ⊗⊗⊗

f. Br^{-}: 4s ⊗ 4p ⊗⊗⊗

g. Mg^{2+}: 2s ⊗ 2p ⊗⊗⊗

h. S^{2-}: 3s ⊗ 3p ⊗⊗⊗

Bonding Reactions: pp. 28–29

(Note: Electron dot formulas below may not represent bond types actually formed in some cases.)

1.  $\Delta E_n = 1.9$

2.  $\Delta E_n = 3.2$

3. 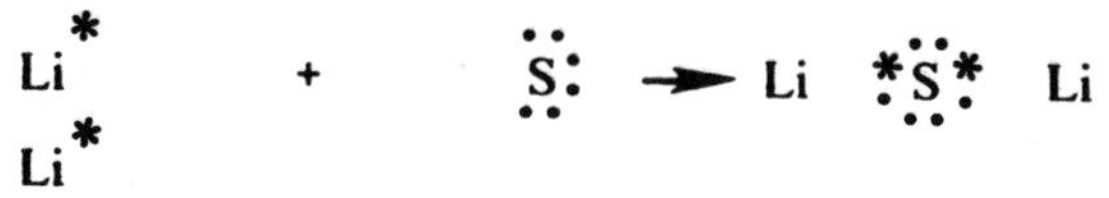 $\Delta E_n = 1.4$

4. 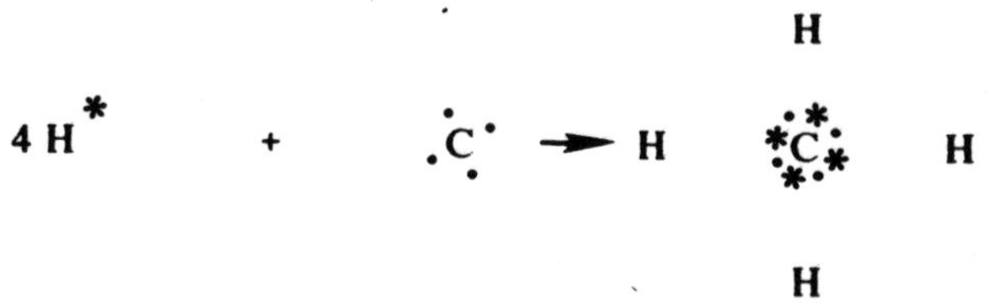 $\Delta E_n = 0.4$

5. 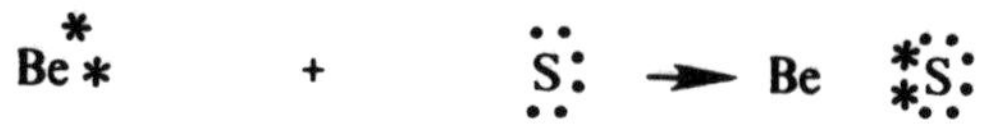 $\Delta E_n = 0.9$

6. 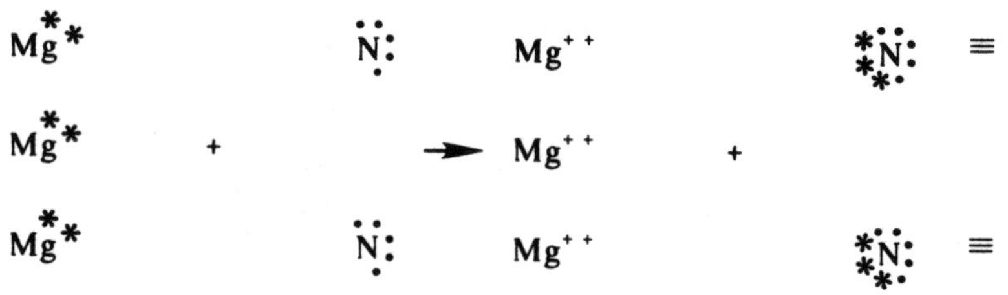 $\Delta E_n = 1.8$

7. 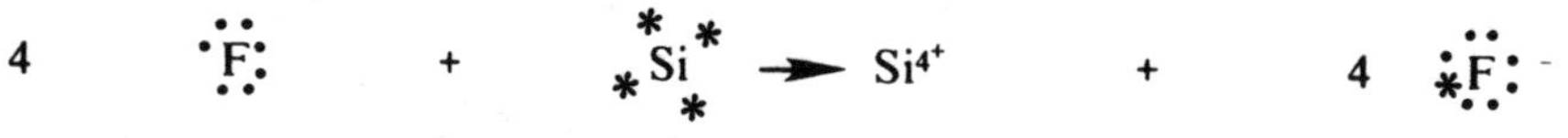 $\Delta E_n = 2.3$

8. 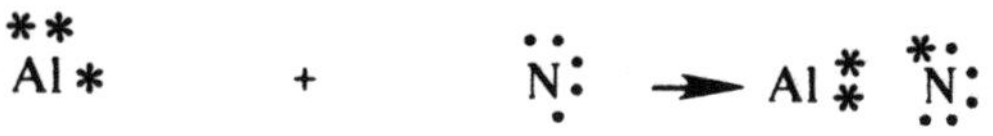 $\Delta E_n = 1.6$

(continued)

9. 4 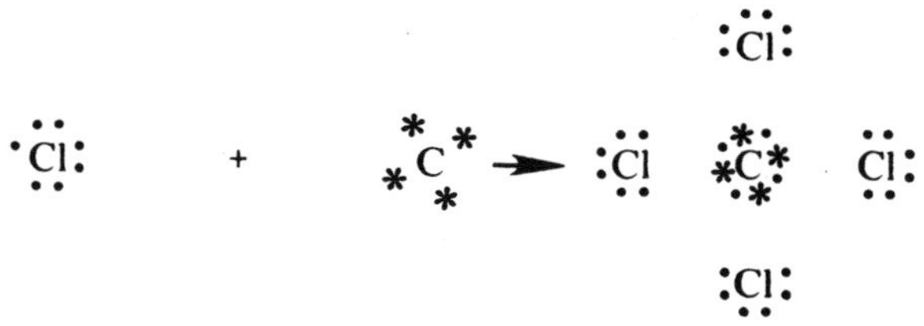 $\Delta E_n = 0.4$

10. 4 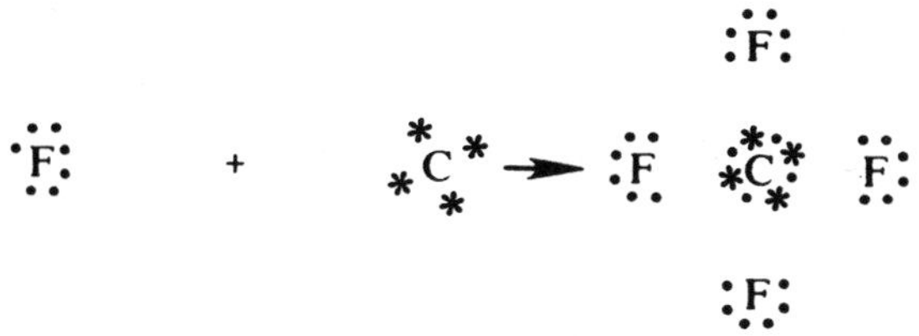 $\Delta E_n = 1.6$

11.  $\Delta E_n = 1.1$

12. 4 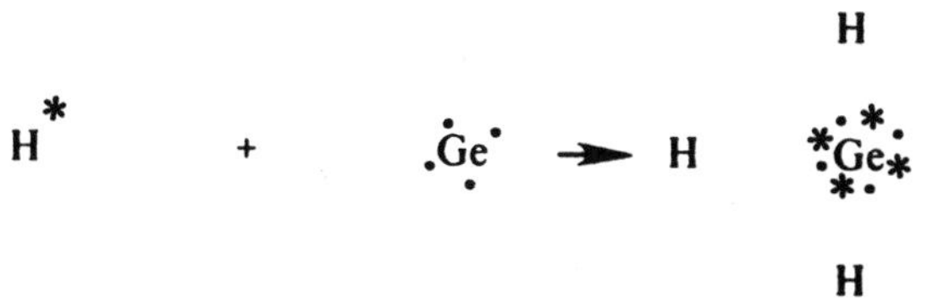 $\Delta E_n = 0.1$

13. 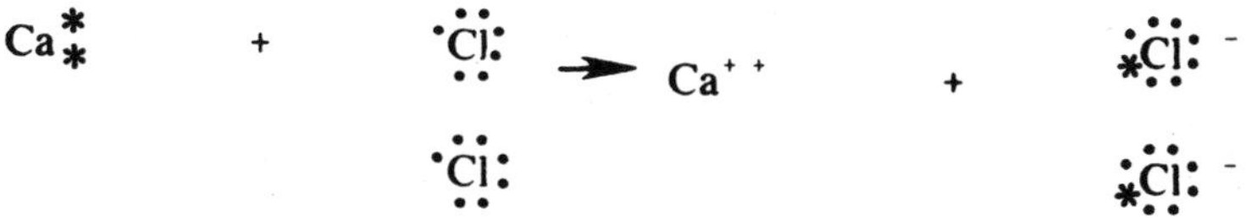 $\Delta E_n = 1.8$

14. 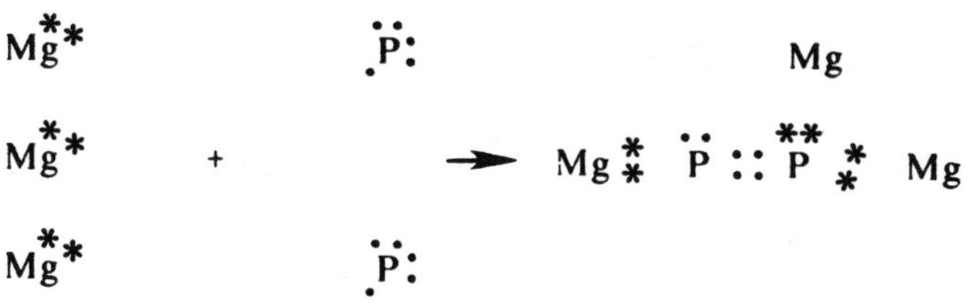 $\Delta E_n = 0.8$

15. 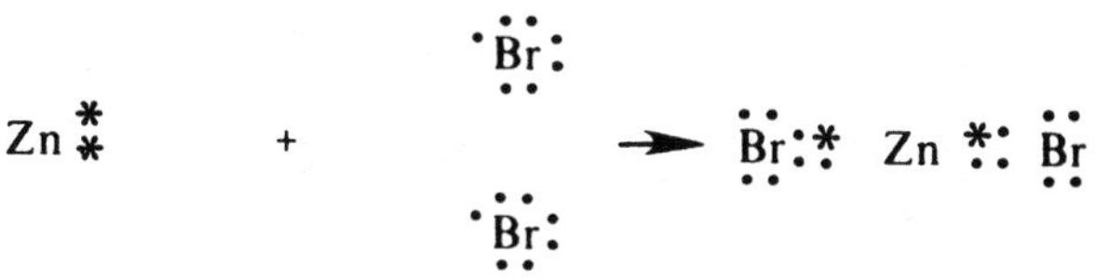 $\Delta E_n = 1.1$

Formulas and Nomenclature: pp. 30–35

Group I.

1. hydrogen chloride or hydrochloric acid
2. potassium hydroxide
3. mercury(I) hydroxide or mercurous hydroxide
4. potassium chloride
5. iron(III) chloride or ferric chloride
6. nitric acid or hydrogen nitrate
7. ammonium hydroxide
8. copper(I) oxide or cuprous oxide
9. aluminum sulfate
10. dinitrogen pentoxide
11. sodium hydroxide
12. carbon dioxide
13. hydrofluoric acid or hydrogen fluoride
14. lead(II) hydroxide or plumbous hydroxide
15. ammonium nitrate
16. sodium bicarbonate or sodium hydrogen carbonate
17. mercury(II) oxide or mercuric oxide
18. zinc nitrite
19. phosphoric acid or hydrogen phosphate
20. cesium hydroxide
21. lithium oxide
22. calcium hydroxide
23. calcium bromide
24. iron(III) oxide or ferric oxide
25. sulfuric acid or hydrogen sulfate
26. iron(II) carbonate or ferrous carbonate
27. sulfur trioxide
28. barium bromate
29. aluminum hydroxide
30. perchloric acid or hydrogen perchlorate
31. sodium acetate
32. sodium sulfite
33. carbonic acid or hydrogen carbonate
34. fluorous acid or hydrogen fluorite
35. ammonium iodate
36. lithium hydride
37. carbon monoxide
38. magnesium bromide
39. tin (IV) bromide or stannic bromide
40. nitrous oxide
41. ammonium fluoride

(continued)

43. potassium bicarbonate
44. potassium oxide
45. barium arsenide
46. zinc oxide
47. sodium hypochlorite
48. strontium sulfide
49. aluminum bromate
50. antimony trifluoride
51. palladium cyanide
52. zinc silicate
53. magnesium acetate
54. calcium permanganate
55. beryllium nitrate
56. nickel selenate
57. radium bromide
58. sodium permanganate
59. lead(II) iodide or plumbous iodide
60. calcium sulfide
61. bismuth telluride
62. potassium perchlorate
63. mercury(II) bromide or mercuric bromide
64. cobalt silicide
65. triphosphorus pentanitride
66. copper(II) sulfite or cupric sulfite
67. iron(III) phosphate or ferric phosphate
68. lead(II) telluride or plumbous telluride
69. mercury(I) nitrate or mercurous nitrate
70. potassium silicate
71. silver acetate
72. tellurium tetraiodide
73. zinc phosphate
74. silver sulfide
75. cadmium bicarbonate
76. zinc fluoride
77. sulfurous acid or hydrogen sulfite
78. barium hydroxide
79. lead(II) sulfide or plumbous sulfide
80. sodium dihydrogen phosphate or monobasic sodium phosphate
81. ammonium acetate
82. silver nitride
83. silicon tetraiodide
84. zinc carbonate
85. phosphorus acid or hydrogen phosphite

(continued)

86. tin(IV) iodide or stannic iodide
87. lead(II) nitrate or plumbous nitrate
88. sodium fluoride
89. potassium aluminum sulfate
90. potassium uranate
91. samarium chloride
92. potassium pentasulfide
93. iron(II) ferricyanide or ferrous ferricyanide
94. platinum(II) chloride or platinous chloride
95. platinum (IV) iodide or platinic iodide
96. nitrogen triiodide
97. molybdenum pentachloride
98. lanthanum nitrate
99. dysprosium oxide
100. vanadium pentoxide

Group II.

1. H_2SO_4
2. NaOH
3. NaBr
4. $Ba(OH)_2$
5. CaO
6. H_2S
7. Li_2SO_4
8. CO
9. MnO_2
10. SO_2
11. $FeSO_4$
12. HClO
13. $KMnO_4$
14. AgCl
15. $Cu(OH)_2$
16. $(NH_4)_2S$
17. $NiBr_2$
18. FeO
19. $HBrO_3$
20. NH_4HSO_4
21. Hg_2SO_4
22. Fe_2O_3
23. $Mg_3(PO_4)_2$
24. $Ni(HCO_3)_2$
25. $Zn(OH)_2$
26. HI
27. P_2O_5
28. $AlPO_4$
29. $HC_2H_3O_2$
30. $Cu(NO_2)_2$
31. NO_2
32. PCl_3
33. Na_3PO_4
34. K_2CO_3
35. H_3PO_4
36. $PbCl_4$
37. $SnBr_2$
38. NH_4OH
39. HIO_4
40. $Fe(OH)_2$
41. CO_2
42. N_2O_5
43. Ag_2O
44. AlN
45. $Mn(OH)_2$
46. $(NH_4)_2CO_3$
47. Al_2O_3
48. Sb_2S_5
49. $BaCO_3$
50. $Ca_3(PO_4)_2$
51. Cs_2CO_3
52. K_2SiO_3
53. Ag_2CrO_4
54. $MgSO_3$
55. CrP
56. $Co(NO_3)_2$
57. ZnI_2
58. FeF_2
59. NiSe
60. $NaHSO_4$
61. Li_2O
62. Cu_2CO_3
63. $SrCO_3$
64. Hg_2SO_4
65. $K_2Cr_2O_7$
66. MnO
67. $NiCl_2$
68. $Pb(C_2H_3O_2)_2$
69. Hg_3N_2
70. $Pb(OH)_2$
71. $SnCl_4$
72. SeF_4
73. PBr_5
74. $HgIO_3$
75. $Fe_2(SO_4)_3$
76. $NiSO_4$
77. SiO_2
78. Li_3PO_4
79. K_3Sb
80. HNO_3
81. Mg_3N_2
82. $Cd(NO_2)_2$
83. $Zn(C_2H_3O_2)_2$
84. HNO_2
85. $Sr(OH)_2$
86. $PbSO_4$
87. $Al(HSO_4)_3$
88. Na_2HPO_4
89. $NH_4Al(SO_4)_2$
90. $CuSO_4 \cdot 5H_2O$
91. $Pb(NO_3)_2$
92. $AuCl_3$
93. $Sn(OH)_2$
94. H_2CO_3
95. NH_4BrO_3
96. $ScBr_3$
97. BrI
98. Rb_2CO_3
99. $K_2S_2O_3$
100. K_3AsO_4

(continued)

101. $KAg(CN)_2$
102. $NaCNO$
103. $HMnO_4$
104. $OsCl_4$
105. La_2O_3
106. $GeCl_4$
107. $Er(C_2H_3O_2)_3$
108. Yb_2O_3
109. CaH_2
110. $Fe_3[Fe(CN)_6]_2$

Equations: pp. 36–44

1. $Fe + S \rightarrow FeS$
2. $Zn + CuSO_4 \rightarrow ZnSO_4 + Cu$
3. $AgNO_3 + NaBr \rightarrow NaNO_3 + AgBr$
4. $2KClO_3 \xrightarrow{\Delta} 2KCl + 3O_2\uparrow$
5. $2H_2O \xrightarrow{\sim} 2H_2 + O_2\uparrow$
6. $2HgO \xrightarrow{\Delta} 2Hg + O_2\uparrow$
7. $2KI + Pb(NO_3)_2 \rightarrow PbI_2 + 2KNO_3$
8. $4Al + 3O_2 \rightarrow 2Al_2O_3$
9. $MgCl_2 + 2NH_4NO_3 \rightarrow Mg(NO_3)_2 + 2NH_4Cl$
10. $FeCl_3 + 3NH_4OH \rightarrow Fe(OH)_3 + 3NH_4Cl$
11. $2Na_2O_2 + 2H_2O \rightarrow 4NaOH + O_2\uparrow$
12. $Fe_2O_3 + 3C \rightarrow 2Fe + 3CO\uparrow$
13. $2Fe + 3H_2O \rightarrow 3H_2\uparrow + Fe_2O_3$
14. $FeCl_3 + 3KOH \rightarrow 3KCl + Fe(OH)_3$
15. $2Al + 3H_2SO_4 \rightarrow Al_2(SO_4)_3 + 3H_2\uparrow$
16. $Na_2CO_3 + Ca(OH)_2 \rightarrow 2NaOH + CaCO_3$
17. $CO_2 + H_2O \rightarrow H_2CO_3$
18. $4P + 5O_2 \rightarrow 2P_2O_5$
19. $2Na + 2HOH \rightarrow 2NaOH + H_2\uparrow$
20. $Zn + H_2SO_4 \rightarrow ZnSO_4 + H_2\uparrow$
21. $Al_2(SO_4)_3 + 3Ca(OH)_2 \rightarrow 2Al(OH)_3 + 3CaSO_4$
22. $CaO + H_2O \rightarrow Ca(OH)_2$
23. $Fe + 2CuNO_3 \rightarrow Fe(NO_3)_2 + 2Cu$
24. $FeS + 2HCl \rightarrow H_2S\uparrow + FeCl_2$
25. $K_2O + H_2O \rightarrow 2KOH$
26. $(NH_4)_2S + Pb(NO_3)_2 \rightarrow 2NH_4NO_3 + PbS$
27. $3Hg(OH)_2 + 2H_3PO_4 \rightarrow Hg_3(PO_4)_2 + 6H_2O$
28. $3KOH + H_3PO_4 \rightarrow K_3PO_4 + 3H_2O$
29. $CaCl_2 + 2\ HNO_3 \rightarrow Ca(NO_3)_2 + 2\ HCl$
30. $K_2CO_3 + BaCl_2 \rightarrow 2KCl + BaCO_3$
31. $Mg(OH)_2 + H_2SO_4 \rightarrow MgSO_4 + 2H_2O$
32. $SO_2 + H_2O \rightarrow H_2SO_3$
33. $Na_2CO_3 + 2HCl \rightarrow 2NaCl + H_2O + CO_2\uparrow$
34. $Mg + 2HNO_3 \rightarrow Mg(NO_3)_2 + H_2\uparrow$
35. $2Al + Fe_2O_3 \rightarrow Al_2O_3 + 2Fe$
36. $2K_3PO_4 + 3MgCl_2 \rightarrow Mg_3(PO_4)_2 + 6KCl$
37. $4NH_3 + 3O_2 \rightarrow 2N_2\uparrow + 6H_2O$

(continued)

38. $CaCO_3 \rightarrow CaO + CO_2 \uparrow$
39. $2NaCl + H_2SO_4 \rightarrow Na_2SO_4 + 2HCl$
40. $2F_2 + 4NaOH \rightarrow 4NaF + O_2 \uparrow + 2H_2O$
41. $Mg(NO_3)_2 + CaI_2 \rightarrow Ca(NO_3)_2 + MgI_2$
42. $Al_2(SO_4)_3 + 6NH_4Br \rightarrow 2AlBr_3 + 3(NH_4)_2SO_4$
43. $2KF + BaBr_2 \rightarrow BaF_2 + 2KBr$
44. $Cu(NO_3)_2 + 2NH_4OH \rightarrow Cu(OH)_2 + 2NH_4NO_3$
45. $2NaNO_3 \rightarrow 2NaNO_2 + O_2 \uparrow$
46. $Pb(OH)_2 \rightarrow PbO + H_2O$
47. $2NH_3 + H_2SO_4 \rightarrow (NH_4)_2SO_4$
48. $HCl + NH_3 \rightarrow NH_4Cl$
49. $CuSO_4 + Fe \rightarrow FeSO_4 + Cu$
50. $2Al + 6HCl \rightarrow 2AlCl_3 + 3H_2 \uparrow$
51. $C + O_2 \rightarrow CO_2 \uparrow$
52. $Ca(HCO_3)_2 + Ca(OH)_2 \rightarrow 2CaCO_3 + 2H_2O$
53. $2H_2S + O_2 \rightarrow 2H_2O + 2S$
54. $2NaOH + Ca(NO_3)_2 \rightarrow 2NaNO_3 + Ca(OH)_2$
55. $2KI + Cl_2 \rightarrow 2KCl + I_2$
56. $H_2SO_4 + 2KOH \rightarrow K_2SO_4 + 2H_2O$
57. $CO_2 + C \rightarrow 2CO \uparrow$
58. $CaSO_4 + Na_2CO_3 \rightarrow CaCO_3 + Na_2SO_4$
59. $3H_2O + P_2O_5 \rightarrow 2H_3PO_4$
60. $2Al + 2H_3PO_4 \rightarrow 3H_2 \uparrow + 2AlPO_4$
61. $NH_4Cl + NaNO_2 \rightarrow NaCl + N_2 \uparrow + H_2O$
62. $Cl_2 + 2NaOH \rightarrow NaCl + NaClO + H_2O$
63. $2Pb(NO_3)_2 \rightarrow 2PbO + 4NO_2 \uparrow + O_2 \uparrow$
64. $2Hg_2O + O_2 \rightarrow 4HgO$
65. $CaO + MgCl_2 \rightarrow MgO + CaCl_2$
66. $Ca + 2H_2O \rightarrow Ca(OH)_2 + H_2 \uparrow$
67. $2CrCl_3 + 3H_2SO_4 \rightarrow Cr_2(SO_4)_3 + 6HCl$
68. $Fe(NO_3)_3 + 3NH_4OH \rightarrow Fe(OH)_3 + 3NH_4NO_3$
69. $AlCl_3 + K_3PO_4 \rightarrow AlPO_4 + 3KCl$
70. $Al_2O_3 + 3C + 3Cl_2 \rightarrow 3CO \uparrow + 2AlCl_3$
71. $Cu_2O + 2HCl \rightarrow 2CuCl + H_2O$
72. $Mg(HCO_3)_2 + 2HCl \rightarrow MgCl_2 + 2H_2O + 2CO_2 \uparrow$
73. $4Fe + 3O_2 \rightarrow 2Fe_2O_3$
74. $Si + 2H_2O \xrightarrow{\Delta} SiO_2 + 2H_2 \uparrow$
75. $Fe_2O_3 + 3CO \rightarrow 2Fe + 3CO_2 \uparrow$
76. $3CaCl_2 + 2Cr(NO_3)_3 \rightarrow 3Ca(NO_3)_2 + 2CrCl_3$
77. $2ZnS + 3O_2 \rightarrow 2ZnO + 2SO_2 \uparrow$
78. $Ca_3(PO_4)_2 + 3H_2SO_4 \rightarrow 3CaSO_4 + 2H_3PO_4$
79. $2Fe(OH)_3 \xrightarrow{\Delta} Fe_2O_3 + 3H_2O$
80. $Al_2S_3 + 6NaHCO_3 \rightarrow 2Al(OH)_3 + 3Na_2SO_4 + 6CO_2 \uparrow$

(continued)

81. $Ca_3(PO_4)_2 + 3SiO_2 + 5C \rightarrow 2P + 3CaSiO_3 + 5CO\uparrow$
82. $CaO + SO_2 \rightarrow CaSO_3$
83. $CO_2 + Mg(OH)_2 \rightarrow MgCO_3 + H_2O$
84. $CaO + 2HCl \rightarrow CaCl_2 + H_2O$
85. $CaCO_3 + SiO_2 \rightarrow CaSiO_3 + CO_2\uparrow$
86. $2Sb + 3Cl_2 \rightarrow 2SbCl_3$
87. $Mg_3N_2 + 6H_2O \rightarrow 3Mg(OH)_2 + 2NH_3\uparrow$
88. $4As + 3O_2 \rightarrow 2As_2O_3$
89. $NH_4HCO_3 \xrightarrow{\Delta} NH_3\uparrow + H_2O\uparrow + CO_2\uparrow$
90. $3CuO + 2NH_3 \rightarrow 3Cu + 3H_2O + N_2\uparrow$
91. $(NH_4)_2Cr_2O_7 \xrightarrow{\Delta} Cr_2O_3 + N_2\uparrow + 4H_2O$
92. $H_2S + Cd(NO_3)_2 \rightarrow 2HNO_3 + CdS$
93. $3BaBr_2 + 2Na_3PO_4 \rightarrow Ba_3(PO_4)_2 + 6NaBr$
94. $AlCl_3 + 3NH_4F \rightarrow AlF_3 + 3NH_4Cl$
95. $2AgNO_3 + K_2SO_4 \rightarrow Ag_2SO_4 + 2KNO_3$
96. $2Bi(NO_3)_3 + 3CaI_2 \rightarrow 2BiI_3 + 3Ca(NO_3)_2$
97. $Al_2(CrO_4)_3 + 3(NH_4)_2SO_4 \rightarrow 3(NH_4)_2CrO_4 + Al_2(SO_4)_3$
98. $Zn(NO_3)_2 + 2NH_4Br \rightarrow ZnBr_2 + 2NH_4NO_3$
99. $Bi(NO_3)_3 + 3NH_4OH \rightarrow Bi(OH)_3 + 3NH_4NO_3$
100. $Cd(NO_3)_2 + H_2SO_4 \rightarrow CdSO_4 + 2HNO_3$
101. $Zn + 2AgI \rightarrow ZnI_2 + 2Ag$
102. $2FeCl_3 + 3H_2SO_4 \rightarrow Fe_2(SO_4)_3 + 6HCl$
103. $Bi_2(SO_4)_3 + 6NH_4OH \rightarrow 2Bi(OH)_3 + 3(NH_4)_2SO_4$
104. $4HI + O_2 \rightarrow 2I_2 + 2H_2O$
105. $K_2SO_4 + BaCl_2 \rightarrow BaSO_4 + 2KCl$
106. $BaSO_4 + 4C \rightarrow BaS + 4CO\uparrow$
107. $Al_2O_3 + 6HF \rightarrow 2AlF_3 + 3H_2O$
108. $2AlF_3 + 3H_2SO_4 \rightarrow Al_2(SO_4)_3 + 6HF\uparrow$
109. $2KI + H_2O_2 \rightarrow 2KOH + I_2$
110. $Zn + Fe_2(SO_4)_3 \rightarrow ZnSO_4 + 2FeSO_4$
111. $PbS + 2PbO \rightarrow 3Pb + SO_2\uparrow$
112. $Cu + 2H_2SO_4 \rightarrow CuSO_4 + 2H_2O + SO_2\uparrow$
113. $2Al(OH)_3 \rightarrow Al_2O_3 + 3H_2O$
114. $N_2 + 3H_2 \rightarrow 2NH_3\uparrow$
115. $Na_2CO_3 + H_2CO_3 \rightarrow 2NaHCO_3$
116. $SiO_2 + 4HF \rightarrow 2H_2O + SiF_4\uparrow$
117. $3NaClO \rightarrow 2NaCl + NaClO_3$
118. $2NaClO_2 + Cl_2 \rightarrow 2NaCl + 2ClO_2\uparrow$
119. $CH_4 + SO_2 \xrightarrow{\Delta} H_2S\uparrow + CO_2\uparrow + H_2\uparrow$
120. $H_2TeO_3 \rightarrow TeO_2\uparrow + H_2O$
121. $FeSe + 2HCl \rightarrow FeCl_2 + H_2Se\uparrow$
122. $3Mg + N_2 \rightarrow Mg_3N_2$
123. $AgCN + K \rightarrow KCN + Ag$

(continued)

124. $CuSO_4 + 4NH_3 \rightarrow Cu(NH_3)_4SO_4$
125. $CaC_2 + N_2 \rightarrow CaCN_2 + C$
126. $CaCN_2 + 3H_2O \rightarrow CaCO_3 + 2NH_3 \uparrow$
127. $Zn_3As_2 + 6HCl \rightarrow 2AsH_3 \uparrow + 3ZnCl_2$
128. $Pb(OH)_2 + Na_2SnO_2 \rightarrow Pb + Na_2SnO_3 + H_2O$
129. $Na_2SiO_3 + 2HCl \rightarrow 2NaCl + H_2SiO_3$
130. $B_2O_3 + 3Mg \rightarrow 3MgO + 2B$
131. $Fe(CN)_2 + 4KCN \rightarrow K_4Fe(CN)_6$
132. $NaAlO_2 + NH_4Cl + NH_4AlO_2 + NaCl$
133. $Al(OH)_3 + 3NaOH \rightarrow Na_3AlO_3 + 3H_2O$
134. $W + 3Cl_2 \xrightarrow{\Delta} WCl_6$
135. $3Ca + 2NH_3 \rightarrow 3CaH_2 + N_2 \uparrow$
136. $Na_2WO_4 + H_2SO_4 \rightarrow Na_2SO_4 + H_2WO_4$
137. $LiH + H_2O \rightarrow LiOH + H_2 \uparrow$
138. $4H_3BO_3 \rightarrow H_2B_4O_7 + 5H_2O$
139. $Zn(OH)_2 + 2KOH \rightarrow K_2ZnO_2 + 2H_2O$
140. $Ni + 4CO \rightarrow Ni(CO)_4$.

Reaction Prediction: pp. 45–51

In the following problems, the answers are given in this order:

a. Type of reaction: S = synthesis; D = decomposition; SR = single replacement; DR = double replacement
b. Yes or no, as to whether the reaction occurs
c. Balanced equation for those that do

For double replacement reactions, any ***product*** listed in Appendix L as P, I, A, or a is regarded as insoluble; any ***reactant*** listed as P is regarded as soluble.

1. SR; yes; $2Al + 6HCl \rightarrow 2AlCl_3 + 3H_2$
2. DR; yes; $Ca(OH)_2 + 2HNO_3 \rightarrow Ca(NO_3)_2 + 2H_2O$
3. S; no
4. SR; yes; $Mg + Zn(NO_3)_2 \rightarrow Mg(NO_3)_2 + Zn \downarrow$
5. S; yes; $2Hg + O_2 \rightarrow 2HgO$
6. DR; yes; $ZnCl_2 + H_2S \rightarrow 2HCl + ZnS \downarrow$
7. S; yes; $N_2O_5 + H_2O \rightarrow 2NHO_3$
8. DR; no; $AgCl \downarrow$
9. D; yes; $2NaClO_3 \xrightarrow{\Delta} 2NaCl + 3O_2 \uparrow$
10. DR; yes; $Ba(NO_3)_2 + Na_2CrO_4 \rightarrow BaCrO_4 \downarrow + 2NaNO_3$
11. DR; yes; $NaBr + AgNO_3 \rightarrow NaNO_3 + AgBr \downarrow$
12. DR; yes; $Ca_3(PO_4)_2 + Al_2(SO_4)_3 \rightarrow 3CaSO_4 + 2AlPO_4 \downarrow$
13. D; yes; $ZnCO_3 \rightarrow ZnO + CO_2 \uparrow$
14. DR; yes; $Hg_2SO_4 + 2NH_4NO_3 \rightleftharpoons (NH_4)_2SO_4 + 2HgNO_3$
15. S; yes; $2K + F_2 \rightarrow 2KF$

(continued)

16. DR; no; $Zn_3(PO_4)_2 \downarrow$
17. S; yes; $Li_2O + H_2O \rightarrow 2LiOH$
18. D; yes; $2NaCl \xrightarrow{\sim} 2Na + Cl_2 \uparrow$
19. S; no
20. DR; yes; $Fe(OH)_3 + H_3PO_4 \rightarrow FePO_4 \downarrow + 3H_2O$
21. SR; yes; $2Na + 2HNO_3 \rightarrow 2NaNO_3 + H_2 \uparrow$
22. DR; yes; $2FeI_3 + 3Cu(NO_3)_2 \rightarrow 2Fe(NO_3)_3 + 3CuI_2$ (decomposes in water)
23. SR; no
24. SR; no
25. S; yes; $SO_2 + H_2O \rightleftharpoons H_2SO_3$
26. S; yes; $S + O_2 \rightarrow SO_2 \uparrow$
27. DR; yes; $Na_2SO_4 + BaCl_2 \rightarrow BaSO_4 \downarrow + 2NaCl$
28. DR; yes; $(NH_4)_3PO_4 + 3LiOH \rightarrow Li_3PO_4 + 3NH_4OH$ $(\rightarrow 3NH_3 \uparrow + 3H_2O)$
29. S; yes; $2H_2 + O_2 \rightarrow 2H_2O$
30. SR; no
31. S; yes; $Na_2O + H_2O \rightarrow 2NaOH$
32. DR; yes; $CaCO_3 + 2LiCl \rightleftharpoons Li_2CO_3 + CaCl_2$
33. DR; yes; $Hg_2SO_4 + 2HCl \rightleftharpoons H_2SO_4 + 2HgCl$
34. D; yes; $2KNO_3 \rightarrow 2KNO_2 + O_2 \uparrow$
35. S; may occur under certain conditions; $Cl_2 + Br_2 \rightarrow 2BrCl$
36. DR; yes; $2HgNO_3 + Na_2CO_3 \rightarrow 2NaNO_3 + Hg_2CO_3 \downarrow$
37. SR; yes; $Mg + 2HCl \rightarrow MgCl_2 + H_2 \uparrow$
38. D; yes; $2H_2O \xrightarrow{\sim} 2H_2 \uparrow + O_2 \uparrow$
39. DR; yes; $2NH_4NO_2 + Ba(OH)_2 \rightarrow 2NH_4OH(\rightarrow 2NH_3 \uparrow + 2H_2O) + Ba(NO_2)_2$
40. DR; yes; $(NH_4)_2SO_4 + Ca(OH)_2 \rightarrow 2NH_4OH (2NH_3 \uparrow + 2H_2O) + CaSO_4$
41. D; yes; $2HgO \rightarrow 2Hg + O_2 \uparrow$
42. DR; yes; $(NH_4)_3PO_4 + AlCl_3 \rightarrow AlPO_4 \downarrow + 3NH_4Cl$
43. S; yes; $BaO + H_2O \rightarrow Ba(OH)_2$
44. DR; yes; $Fe(OH)_3 + 3HNO_3 \rightarrow Fe(NO_3)_3 + 3H_2O$
45. S; yes; $2Ca + O_2 \rightarrow 2CaO$
46. SR; yes; $3Ca + 2H_3PO_4 \rightarrow Ca_3(PO_4)_2 + 3H_2 \uparrow$
47. DR; yes; $CaCl_2 + 2NH_4OH \rightleftharpoons Ca(OH)_2 + 2NH_4Cl$
48. DR; yes; provided the Al_2S_3 is added as a solid; Al_2S_3 does not exist in water solution;
    $Al_2S_3 + 6HCl \rightarrow 2AlCl_3 + 3H_2S \uparrow$
49. S; yes; $Mg + S \rightarrow MgS$
50. SR; yes; $3Ca + 2AlCl_3 \rightarrow 3CaCl_2 + 2Al$
51. DR; yes; $2KOH + H_2S \rightarrow 2H_2O + K_2S$
52. DR; yes; $Na_2CO_3 + H_2SO_4 \rightarrow Na_2SO_4 + H_2CO_3(H_2O + CO_2 \uparrow)$
53. DR; no; $BaSO_4 \downarrow$
54. SR; no
55. D; yes; $BaCO_3 \xrightarrow{\Delta} BaO + CO_2 \uparrow$
56. S; yes; $2Li + Br_2 \rightarrow 2LiBr$
57. DR; yes; $2NaCl + K_2CrO_4 \rightleftharpoons Na_2CrO_4 + 2KCl$

(continued)

58. DR; yes; $K_2S + Fe(NO_3)_2 \rightarrow FeS\downarrow + 2KNO_3$
59. SR; no
60. S; no
61. D; yes; $2AlCl_3 \xrightarrow{\sim} 2Al + 3Cl_2\uparrow$
62. DR; yes; $Pb(ClO_3)_2 + Na_2S \rightarrow PbS\downarrow + 2NaClO_3$
63. S; yes, although there are practical difficulties; $SO_3 + H_2O \rightarrow H_2SO_4$
64. DR; yes; $CaCO_3 + 2HCl \rightarrow CaCl_2 + H_2CO_3\ (\rightarrow H_2O + CO_2\uparrow)$
65. SR; no
66. DR; yes; $2NH_4C_2H_3O_2 + FeCl_2 \rightleftharpoons 2NH_4Cl + Fe(C_2H_3O_2)_2$
67. DR; no; $AgBr\downarrow$
68. SR; yes; $Zn + H_2SO_4 \rightarrow ZnSO_4 + H_2\uparrow$
69. S; no
70. SR; no
71. DR; yes; $Pb(OH)_2 + 2HCl \rightarrow PbCl_2 + 2H_2O$
72. S; yes; $Fe + S \rightarrow FeS$
73. D; yes; $2KClO_3 \xrightarrow{\Delta} 3O_2\uparrow + 2KCl$
74. S; under special circumstances, yes; $Cl_2 + 2O_2 \rightarrow 2ClO_2$
75. DR; no; $AgI\downarrow$
76. DR; yes; $3FeCO_3 + 2H_3PO_4 \rightarrow Fe_3(PO_4)_2\downarrow + 3H_2CO_3\ (\rightarrow 3H_2O + 3CO_2\uparrow)$
77. DR; yes; $KI + NH_4NO_3 \rightleftharpoons KNO_3 + NH_4I$
78. SR; yes; $K + NaNO_3 \rightarrow Na + KNO_3$
79. SR; no
80. DR; yes; $Ag_2S + 2HCl \rightarrow 2AgCl\downarrow + H_2S\uparrow$
81. DR; yes; $Mg(NO_3)_2 + 2HCl \rightleftharpoons 2NHO_3 + MgCl_2$
82. S; yes; $NH_3 + HCl \rightarrow NH_4Cl$
83. DR; yes; $Zn(OH)_2 + H_2SO_4 \rightarrow ZnSO_4 + 2H_2O$
84. S; yes; $CaO + H_2O \rightarrow Ca(OH)_2$
85. S; yes; $2Na + Cl_2 \rightarrow 2NaCl$
86. D; yes; $Ca(OH)_2 \xrightarrow{\Delta} CaO + H_2O$
87. SR; yes; $F_2 + 2KBr \rightarrow 2KF + Br_2$
88. DR; yes; $2NH_4OH + H_2SO_4 \rightarrow (NH_4)_2SO_4 + 2H_2O$
89. DR; yes; $NaCl + KNO_3 \rightleftharpoons NaNO_3 + KCl$
90. SR; no
91. S; yes; $CO_2 + H_2O \rightleftharpoons H_2CO_3$
92. SR; yes; $Cl_2 + 2LiBr \rightarrow 2LiCl + Br_2$
93. DR; yes; $3LiOH + H_3PO_4 \rightarrow Li_3PO_4 + 3H_2O$
94. DR; yes; $K_2SO_3 + 2HNO_3 \rightarrow 2KNO_3 + H_2SO_3\ (\rightarrow H_2O + SO_2\uparrow)$
95. DR; yes; $NH_4Cl + KOH \rightarrow KCl + NH_4OH(\rightarrow NH_3\uparrow + H_2O)$
96. DR; yes; $SrCO_3 + 2HNO_3 \rightarrow Sr(NO_3)_2 + H_2CO_3\ (\rightarrow H_2O + CO_2\uparrow)$
97. SR; yes; $Sn + 2HgNO_3 \rightarrow Sn(NO_3)_2 + 2Hg$
98. DR; yes; $(NH_4)_2SO_3 + 2HCl \rightarrow 2NH_4Cl + H_2SO_3\ (\rightarrow H_2O + SO_2\uparrow)$
99. DR; yes; $3MgCO_3 + 2H_3PO_4 \rightarrow Mg_3(PO_4)_2 + 3H_2CO_3\ (\rightarrow 3H_2O + 3CO_2\uparrow)$
100. DR; yes; $Al_2(SO_3)_3 + 6HCl \rightarrow 2AlCl_3 + 3H_2SO_3\ (\rightarrow 3H_2O + 3CO_2\uparrow)$

Density and Specific Gravity: pp. 52–55

- SOLIDS AND LIQUIDS

1. 8.9
2. 21.4 g/cm^3, 21.4
3. 11.3 g/cm^3, 11.3
4. 1500 g
5. 0.900
6. 2.7, 2.7 g/cm^3
7. 1200 g
8. 2.70
9. 130 cm^3
10. 50 lb (54.9 lb)
11. 1.3
12. 5300 lb
13. 1.84
14. 0.991 g/cm^3
15. 440 lb/ft^3
16. 100 g (99.7 g)
17. 1260 g
18. 0.920 g/cm^3, 0.920
19. 150 mL
20. 4200 lb

- GAS AND VAPORS

1. 1.639 g/L, 1.268
2. 0.7710 g/L, 0.5963
3. 44.303, 1.5297
4. 1.25 g/L, 28.0
5. 3.21 g/L, 72.1
6. 0.0695, 2.01
7. 3.74 g/L, 2.89, 83.7
8. 10. g
9. 5.61 g/L, 126
10. 4.61 g/L, 3.57, 103
11. 3.165 g/L
12. 3.02, 87.4
13. 1.206 g
14. .554
15. 5.70 g/L, 4.41, 128
16. 5.517
17. 0.586 g
18. 2.72 g/L, 60.8
19. 1.62, 46.8
20. 2.927 g/L, 2.264, 65.56
21. 0.1381, 4.00
22. 0.6830 g
23. 1.341 g/L, 30.03
24. 1.38
25. 1.43 g/L, 1.11, 32.0
26. 1.65 g
27. 1.25 g/L, 0.967
28. 28.6
29. 23.0 g
30. 3.61 g/L, 2.79

Gas Law Problems: pp. 56–63

Group I.

1. 110 mL
2. 330 mL
3. 290 mL
4. 0.98 L
5. 97.37 mL
6. 243.6 mL
7. 38.0 mL
8. 656.3 mL
9. 431 mL
10. 642 mL
11. 74 mL
12. 40 mL
13. 59 mL
14. 32 mL
15. 11 mL
16. 250 mL (252 mL)
17. 240 mL
18. 45 mL (45.1 mL)
19. 140 mL
20. 260 mL
21. 1.7 L
22. 680 mL
23. 18 mL
24. 170 mL
25. 410 mL
26. 14 mL
27. 30. mL
28. 160 mL
29. 52 mL
30. 0.079 L
31. 20. mL
32. 130 mL
33. 81 mL
34. 4.7 L
35. 44 mL
36. 95 mL
37. 6.1 L
38. 82 mL
39. 710 mL
40. 30. L

Group II.

1. 640 mm
2. 54 cm
3. 58 cm
4. 4.4 atm
5. 5000 mm (4980 mm)
6. 860 mm

Group III.

1. −63° C
2. 95° C
3. −28° C
4. 40° C (41° C)
5. −140° C
6. −240° C

Group IV.

1. $1\bar{0}0$ mL
2. 446 mL
3. 220 mL
4. 16 mL
5. 140 mL
6. 730 mm
7. 15 mL
8. 650 mm

Group V.

1. 1.73 g/L
2. 0.16 g/L
3. 1.3 g/L
4. 1.7 g/L
5. 1.1 g/L
6. 1.3 g/L
7. 2.6 g/L
8. 1.1 g/L
9. 3.3 g/L
10. 0.72 g/L
11. 0.090 g/L
12. 2.2 g/L
13. 6.4 g/L
14. 8×10^{-5} g/L (7.85×10^{-5} g/L)
15. 890 g/L
16. 1.7 g/L
17. 1 g/L (1.25 g/L)
18. 0.90 g/L
19. 0.090 g/L
20. 2.0 g/L
21. decreased by 7° C
22. 1700 L
23. 2800 L
24. yes pressure reaches about 3.2 atm
25. 0.88 L
26. increased by 19° C
27. 650 mm
28. 14 L
29. 110° C
30. 150° C

Group VI.

1. 22 atm
2. 82 L
3. 71
4. 227° C
5. 0.15 atm
6. 52
7. 814° C
8. 8.3 mL

Group VII.

1. p_A = 353 mm; p_B = 432 mm
2. p_A = 0.399 atm; p_B = 0.420 atm; p_C = 0.231 atm
3. p_T = 800 torr; m_A = 53%; m_B = 23%; m_C = 25%
4. p_B = 0.69 atm; m_A = 38%; m_B = 62%
5. p_B = 296 torr; p_C = 392 torr; p_T = 871 torr
6. m_{CO_2} = 0.227 mol (29.8%); m_{N_2} = 0.536 mol (70.2%); p_{CO_2} = 0.340 atm; p_{N_2} = 0.802 atm
7. m_{Ar} = 0.125 mol (56.1%); m_{Xe} = 0.038 mol (17.1%); m_{Kr} = 0.060 mol (26.9%); p_{Xe} = 7.1 torr; p_{Kr} = 41.4 torr
8. m_{SO_2} = 5.3×10^{-5} mol (3.5%); m_{CO_2} = 4.1×10^{-5} mol (2.7%); m_{N_2} = 1.4×10^{-3} mol (93.8%); P_{SO_2} = 0.045 atm; p_{CO_2} = 0.035 atm; p_{N_2} = 1.20 atm

Group VIII.

1. 1 : 3.74
2. 1 : 1.17
3. 1 : 4.69
4. 1 : 1.07
5. 1 : 1.39
6. 1 : 1.25

Group IX.

1. 2.51 g/L
2. 5.33 g/L
3. 2.28 g/L
4. 5.54 g/L
5. 3.88 g/L
6. 3.34 g/L

Molecular Weight and Mole Calculations: pp. 64–67

Group I.

1. 98.00
2. 133.34
3. 213.53
4. 226.28
5. 98.08
6. 108.02
7. 244.66
8. 154.76
9. 186.73
10. 149.12
11. 233.00
12. 64.06
13. 474.44
14. 213.90
15. 191.94
16. 368.37
17. 336.48
18. 307.78
19. 212.27
20. 427.62
21. 183.48
22. 223.16
23. 44.01
24. 162.12
25. 63.02
26. 213.01
27. 132.16
28. 244.27
29. 357.49
30. 121.64
31. 126.06
32. 100.95
33. 36.46
34. 399.88
35. 367.00
36. 168.36
37. 187.57
38. 184.11
39. 106.88
40. 96.11

Group II.

1. 119.00 g
2. 110.98 g
3. 167.96 g
4. 31.01 g
5. 6.90 g
6. 53.50 g
7. 29.17 g
8. 64.45 g
9. 959.92 g
10. 62.47 g
11. 54.8 g
12. 72.1 g
13. 2.4 g
14. 5.15 g
15. 7.56×10^{-3} g
16. 230 g
17. 58.6 g
18. 0.39 g
19. 0.25 g
20. 7.97×10^{-4} g

Group III.

1. 1.000 mol
2. 1.00 mol
3. 0.500 mol
4. 2.000 mol
5. 0.25 mol
6. 0.333 mol
7. 0.176 mol
8. 0.235 mol
9. 0.0970 mol
10. 0.064 mol
11. 0.038 mol
12. 0.019 mol
13. 0.124 mol
14. 0.00102 mol
15. 0.150 mol
16. 7.347×10^{-4} mol
17. 8.18×10^{-7} mol
18. 2.22×10^{-4} mol
19. 0.03968 mol
20. 0.04236 mol

Percentage Composition: pp. 68–70

Answers are given in the same order in which the elements occur in the compound.

1. 39.4%, 60.6%
2. 1.2%, 98.8%
3. 23.5%, 76.5%
4. 42.9%, 57.1%
5. 50.0%, 50.0%
6. 1.5%, 98.5%

(continued)

7. 71.0%, 29.0%
8. 6.6%, 93.4%
9. 82.4%, 17.6%
10. 14.3%, 4.1%, 81.6%
11. 27.0%, 16.5%, 56.5%
12. 2.0%, 32.6%, 65.4%
13. 24.4%, 17.0%, 58.6%
14. 46.8%, 50.0%, 3.2%
15. 55.2%, 14.6%, 30.2%
16. 50.8%, 16.0%, 33.2%
17. 72.4%, 27.6%
18. 21.2%, 6.1%, 24.3%, 48.4%
19. 25.5%, 12.8%, 25.6%, 4.1%, 32.0%
20. 11.1%, 3.2%, 41.3%, 44.4%
21. 32.8%, 67.2%
22. 78.9%, 21.1%
23. 46.7%, 53.3%
24. 0.8%, 99.2%
25. 27.3%, 72.7%
26. 11.1%, 88.9%
27. 74.3%, 25.7%
28. 11.4%, 88.6%
29. 96.0%, 4.0%
30. 45.9%, 16.5%, 37.6%
31. 26.2%, 7.5%, 66.3%
32. 3.1%, 31.6%, 65.3%
33. 80.1%, 18.7%, 1.2%
34. 12.7%, 19.7%, 67.6%
35. 18.0%, 26.8%, 55.2%
36. 38.8%, 20.0%, 41.2%
37. 53.0%, 47.0%
38. 29.1%, 8.3%, 12.5%, 50.1%
39. 28.1%, 8.2%, 20.8%, 42.9%
40. 56.3%, 29.0%, 1.6%, 13.1%
41. 55.3%
42. 12.0%
43. 36.0%
44. 3.8%
45. 40.5%
46. 32.2%
47. 42.1%
48. 72.7%
49. 35.3%
50. 5.9%
51. 72.5 g
52. 100.0 g
53. 405 lb
54. 3.9 g
55. 9.59 g
56. 8.71 g
57. 173.2 lb
58. 19.54 g
59. 56.8 g
60. yes, 19.2 g are produced.

Empirical Formula: pp. 71–72

1. Cu_2O
2. CH_2O
3. CH
4. Fe_2O_3
5. HO
6. CuO
7. K_2CO_3
8. $CHCl_3$
9. $CrCl_2$
10. CS_2
11. NO_2
12. NH_3
13. CH_3O
14. CH_4
15. $CaSO_4$
16. KNO_3
17. MgO
18. Al_2O_3
19. Fe_3O_4
20. $ZnCO_3$
21. As_2S_3
22. $HgCl_2$
23. $TbCl_3$
24. Sc_2O_3
25. GaC_3O_6 (gallium oxalate, $Ga_2(C_2O_4)_3$)
26. K_2SO_4
27. HgO
28. $MgCl_2$
29. $BaCl_2$
30. FeS
31. FeO
32. CaO
33. CO_2
34. $K_2Cr_2O_7$
35. HgO

Molecular Formula: pp. 73–75

Group I.

1. CO_2
2. C_6H_6
3. H_2S
4. S_2Cl_2
5. N_2O_4
6. H_2F_2
7. NO
8. C_2H_4
9. CH_4O
10. $CHCl_3$
11. C_2N_2
12. CO
13. $C_2H_4O_2$
14. C_2H_6
15. $C_{10}H_{14}O_2$

Group II.

1. C_7H_9N
2. $C_4H_6O_2$
3. $C_4H_{10}O$
4. $C_{12}H_{24}O_2$
5. $C_6H_{12}N_4$
6. $C_4H_6O_2$
7. $C_4H_6O_4$
8. $C_6H_8N_2$
9. $C_{10}H_8S_2O_6$
10. $C_{10}H_{14}N_2$
11. $C_6H_2O_8N_2$
12. $C_2H_2O_4$
13. $C_6H_{12}N_2O_4$
14. $C_8H_{16}O_4$
15. $C_6H_{12}O_2$

Stoichiometry: pp. 78–86

- WEIGHT-WEIGHT PROBLEMS

1. 20.5 g of $CaCO_3$; 9.04 g of CO_2; 22.8 g of $CaCl_2$
2. 400.0 g of SO_2
3. 11.7 g of N_2
4. 78.75 lb of CO; 16.88 lb of C; 105.0 lb of Fe with CO; 105.0 lb of Fe with C
5. 75.4 g of H_2SO_4; 56.2 g of HCl; 1.54 g of H_2 formed in either case
6. 500.0 lb of $Ca_3(PO_4)_2$; 561.3 lb of $CaSiO_3$; 290.3 lb of SiO_2
7. 35 g of H_3PO_4; 72 g of $CaSO_4$
8. 74.72 g of PH_3; 243.9 g of $Ca(OH)_2$
9. 45.45 lb of C; 378.8 lb of As
10. 4.94 g of Fe; 7.18 g of Sb
11. 180 tons of boric acid
12. 10.7 g of Ca
13. 26.8 g of $CaCO_3$
14. 19.8 g of $Ca(OH)_2$
15. 19.8 g of $Ca\ (OH)_2$
16. 149 g of $MgSO_4$; 176 g of Na_2SO_4
17. 3.7 g of $Ca(HCO_3)_2$
18. 1.8 g of NaOH
19. 0.78 g of Na_2CO_3
20. 37.2 g of $BeCl_2$; 40.5 g of Na_2BeO_2; 34.0 g of HCl; 37.2 g of NaOH
21. 1.67 g of $TbCl_3$
22. 16.8 μg of $GdCl_3$; 17.0 μg of $EuCl_3$; 17.1 μg of $SmCl_3$
23. 13.79 lb of C; 11.84 lb of C; 6.475 lb of C; 4.444 lb of C; 7.947 lb of C
24. 1.8 kg of $LaCl_3$; 1.8 kg of $CeCl_3$

(continued)

25. 63.94 g of $CuSO_4$
26. 3.7 g of Hg; 4.8 g of $SnCl_4$
27. 7.7 mg of $AuCl_3$; 1.6 mg of HNO_3
28. 2.69 tons of C
29. 16.6 g of AgBr
30. 2177 g of H_2SO_4
31. 21.04 g of NaCl
32. 100 g of KCl (99.78 g)
33. 23.06 g of BaO_2 in xs; 285.3 g of $BaSO_4$
34. 84. g of H_2O; 0.62 g of H_2
35. no; C in excess by 6.2 g
36. 2.3 g of H_2
37. 14.3 g of H_2
38. 11 g of NH_3
39. 44.00 g of CO_2
40. yes
41. yes
42. yes

- WEIGHT-VOLUME PROBLEMS

1. 59 g of FeS
2. 140.0 L of H_2S; 46.67 L of H_2S; 200.0 g of S; 46.67 L of SO_2
3. 14.0 g of MgO; 70.0 g of Mg_3N_2
4. 17.5 L of N_2
5. 710 g of Cu
6. 6.0714 kg of NH_3
7. 4218.8 g of HNO_3
8. 137.1 L of O_2
9. 0.14 L of O_2
10. 187 L of water gas
11. 9.4 g of Li
12. 48.9 g of HCl
13. 40 g of As
14. 43.07 L of H_2F_2
15. 143.0 L of H_2
16. 22.2 L
17. 0.4 L of H_2
18. 161 g of Ca
19. 330.4 g of Ca_3N_2
20. 6.89 L of steam; 6.89 L of H_2

- VOLUME-VOLUME PROBLEMS

1. 50 L of H_2; 100 L of HCl
2. 12 L of O_2; 25 L of CO_2
3. 300 L of H_2; 100 L of N_2
4. 10 L of NO; all N_2 is used; 10 L of O_2 remain
5. H_2 in excess by 20.0 L; 30.0 L of H_2F_2 formed
6. 25.0 L of O_2
7. 7 L per minute
8. 30 per second

- COMBINATIONS

1. 0.44 L of H_2; 2.4 g of VCl_2
2. 40.0 L per second; 104 g NaCl per second; 94.6 g Na_2CO_3 per second; 20.0 L per second of CO_2
3. 78.63 g of Na; 38.29 L of Cl_2
4. 18.4 g of Mg; 17.1 L of H_2
5. 62.2 L of H_2; 31.1 L of O_2
6. 26.019 g of $KClO_3$; 7.1367 L of O_2
7. 8.0 g of C; 15 L of CO_2
8. 6.3 L of Cl_2; 33 g of NaCl
9. 77.7 g of MnO_2; 113 g of $MnCl_2$
10. 0.27 g of Mg; 0.81 g of HCl
11. 2.4 L of O_2; 42 g of Hg
12. 1.194 g NH_4Cl; 500.0 mL of HCl

Ionic Equations: pp. 87–92

NOTE: In the following answers, double and triple positive and negatives charges (e.g., = or ++) can also be written as 2+, 2–, 3+, and 3–.

Group I.

Form: $AB \rightarrow A^+ + B^-$

Group II.

Form: $A_x^{y+}B_y^{x-} \rightarrow {}_xA^{y+} + {}_yB^{x-}$

Group III.

1. H_2S
2. $C_3H_5(OH)_3$
3. $Li^+ Cl^-$
4. $K^+ OH^-$
5. HCN
6. $K_3^+ PO_4^{\equiv}$
7. $Be^{++} (OH)_2^-$
8. $Ca^{++} I_2^-$
9. HCl
10. $K_2^+SO_3^{=}$
11. $NH_4^+Br^-$
12. CCl_4
13. $Ca^{++}(OH)_2^-$
14. $Sr^{++}Br_2^-$
15. Na^+F^-
16. HI
17. $Na^+H_2^+PO_4^{\equiv}$
18. $Na_2^+SO_4^{=}$
19. H_3BO_3
20. $C_{12}H_{22}O_{11}$
21. $Sm^{+++}Br_3^-$
22. H_2Se
23. K^+Br^-
24. CH_4
25. $NH_4^+Cl^-$

Group IV.

1. $Na^+Cl^- \rightarrow Na^+ + Cl^-$
2. $Ba^{++}(OH)_2^- \rightarrow Ba^{++} + 2OH^-$
3. $Ca^{++}Cl_2^- \rightarrow Ca^{++} + 2Cl^-$
4. $HI \rightarrow H^+ + I^-$

(continued)

5. $NH_4^+Br^- \rightarrow NH_4^+ + Br^-$
6. $K_2^+CO_3^= \rightarrow 2K^+ + CO_3^=$
7. $Na^+OH^- \rightarrow Na^+ + OH^-$
8. $HC_7H_5O_2 \rightarrow H^+ + C_7H_5O_2^-$
9. no ionization
10. $Na_3^+PO_4^\equiv \rightarrow 3Na^+ + PO_4^\equiv$
11. $H_2Te \rightarrow 2H^+ + Te^=$
12. $K^+I^- \rightarrow K^+ + I^-$
13. $Sr^{++}(OH)_2^- \rightarrow Sr^{++} + 2OH^-$
14. no ionization
15. $HBr \rightarrow H^+ + Br^-$
16. no ionization
17. $Fe^{++}I_2^- \rightarrow Fe^{++} + 2I^-$
18. $H_2SO_4 \rightarrow 2H^+ + SO_4^=$
19. $Mg^{++}F_2^- \rightarrow Mg^{++} + 2F^-$
20. $Al^{+++}Cl_3 \rightarrow Al^{+++} + 3Cl^-$
21. $Na_2^+H^+PO_4^\equiv \rightarrow 2Na^+ + H^+ + PO_4^\equiv$
22. $HC_2H_3O_2 \rightarrow H^+ + C_2H_3O_2^-$
23. $(NH_4)_2^+SO_4^= \rightarrow 2NH_4^+ + SO_4^=$
24. $Li^+F^- \rightarrow Li^+ + F^-$
25. $HCHO_2 \rightarrow H^+ + CHO_2^-$

Group V.

In the following equations, first the ionic, then the net ionic equation, is given. Compounds listed as P in Appendix L are regarded as soluble when they appear as reactants. Those listed as I, A, a, or P are regarded as insoluble when they appear as products.

1. $K^+ + Cl^- + Na^+ + NO_3^- \rightleftharpoons K^+ + NO_3^- + Na^+ + Cl^-$; NR
2. $Rb^+ + OH^- + H^+ + Cl^- \rightarrow Rb^+ + Cl^- + H_2O$; $OH^- + H^+ \rightarrow H_2O$
3. $Li^+ + ClO_3^- + NH_4^+ + Cl^- \rightleftharpoons Li^+ + Cl^- + NH_4^+ + ClO_3^-$; NR
4. $Ca^{++} + 2\ Cl^- + 2\ Na^+ + CO_3^= \rightarrow 2\ Na^+ + 2\ Cl^- + Ca^{++}CO_3^=\downarrow$; $Ca^{++} + CO_3^= \rightarrow Ca^{++}CO_3^=\downarrow$
5. $Ca^{++} + CO_3^= + 2\ Cs^+ + 2\ Cl^- \rightleftharpoons Ca^{++} + 2\ Cl^- + 2\ Cs^+ + CO_3^=$; NR
6. $2\ NH_4^+ + CO_3^= + 2\ H^+ + 2\ I^- \rightarrow 2\ NH_4^+ + 2\ I^- + H_2CO_3\ (\rightarrow H_2O + CO_2\uparrow)$; $CO_3^= + 2\ H^+ \rightarrow H_2O + CO_2\uparrow$
7. $2\ Al^{+++} + 6\ Br^- + 3\ Cd^{++} + 6\ NO_3^- \rightleftharpoons 2\ Al^{+++} + 6\ NO_3^- + 3\ Cd^{++} + 6\ Br^-$; NR
8. NR; CuI_2 not stable in water solution
9. $2\ Fe^{+++} + 3\ SO_4^= + 3\ Pb^{++} + 6\ ClO_3^- \rightarrow 2\ Fe^{+++} + 6\ ClO_3^- + 3\ Pb^{++}SO_4^=\downarrow$; $3\ SO_4^= + 3\ Pb^{++} \rightarrow 3\ Pb^{++}SO_4^=\downarrow$
10. $2\ Na^+ + 2\ OH^- + 2\ H^+ + SO_4^= \rightarrow 2\ Na^+ + SO_4^= + 2\ H_2O$; $2\ OH^- + 2\ H^+ \rightarrow 2\ H_2O$
11. $Sr^{++} + 2\ Cl^- + 2\ K^+ + SO_4^= \rightarrow 2\ K^+ + 2\ Cl^- + Sr^{++}SO_4^=\downarrow$; $Sr^{++} + SO_4^= \rightarrow Sr^{++}SO_4^=\downarrow$
12. $2\ Hg^+ + 2\ NO_3^- + Ni^{++} + SO_4^= \rightarrow Ni^{++} + 2\ NO_3^- + Hg_2^+SO_4^=\downarrow$; $2\ Hg^+ + SO_4^= \rightarrow Hg_2^+SO_4^=\downarrow$
13. $3\ H^+ + PO_4^\equiv + 3\ NH_4^+ + 3\ OH^- \rightarrow 3\ NH_4^+ + PO_4^= + 3\ H_2O$; $3\ H^+ + 3\ OH^- \rightarrow 3\ H_2O$
14. $K^+ + OH^- + NH_4^+ + Br^- \rightarrow K^+ + Br^- + NH_4OH\ (\rightarrow NH_3\uparrow + H_2O)$; $OH^- + NH_4^+ \rightarrow NH_4OH$ $(\rightarrow NH_3\uparrow + H_2O)$
15. $Cu^{++} + SO_4^= + 2\ Na^+ + 2\ Br^- \rightleftharpoons Cu^{++} + 2\ Br^- + 2\ Na^+ + SO_4^=$; NR
16. $2\ NH_4^+ + 2\ Br^- + Ca^{++} + 2\ OH^- \rightarrow Ca^{++} + 2\ Br^- + 2\ NH_4OH\ (\rightarrow 2\ NH_3\uparrow + 2\ HO_2)$; $2\ NH_4^+ + 2\ OH^- \rightarrow 2\ NH_4OH\ (\rightarrow 2\ NH_3\uparrow + 2\ H_2O)$
17. $Ca^{++} + 2\ NO_3^- + 2\ K^+ + 2\ Cl^- \rightleftharpoons Ca^{++} + 2\ Cl^- + 2\ K^+ + 2\ NO_3^-$; NR
18. $2\ Li^+ + 2\ OH^- + 2\ H^+ + S^= \rightarrow 2\ Li^+ + S^= + 2\ H_2O$; $2\ OH^- + 2\ H^+ \rightarrow 2\ H_2O$
19. $2\ Fe^{+++} + 6\ Cl^- + 6\ Na^+ + 3\ S^= \rightarrow 6\ Na^+ + 6\ Cl^- + Fe_2^{+++}S_3^=\downarrow$; $2\ Fe^{+++} + 3\ S^= \rightarrow Fe_2^{+++}S_3^=\downarrow$
20. $3\ Fe^{++} + 6\ C_2H_3O_2^- + 6\ K^+ + 2\ PO_4^\equiv \rightarrow 6\ K^+ + 6\ C_2H_3O_2^- + Fe_3^{++}(PO_4)_2^\equiv\downarrow$; $3\ Fe^{++} + 2\ PO_4^\equiv \rightarrow Fe_3^{++}(PO_4)_2^\equiv\downarrow$
21. $2\ Na^+ + S^= + 2\ H^+ + 2\ Br^- \rightarrow 2\ Na^+ + 2\ Br^- + H_2S\uparrow$; $S^= + 2\ H^+ \rightarrow H_2S\uparrow$
22. $6\ NH_4^+ + 2\ PO_4^\equiv + 3\ Mg^{++} + 6\ NO_3^- \rightarrow 6\ NH_4^+ + 6\ NO_3^- + Mg_3^{++}(PO_4)_2^\equiv\downarrow$; $3\ Mg^{++} + 2\ PO_4^\equiv \rightarrow Mg_3^{++}(PO_4)_2^\equiv\downarrow$
23. $Ni^{++} + 2\ Cl^- + 2\ Na^+ + CO_3^= \rightarrow 2\ Na^+ + 2\ Cl^- + Ni^{++}CO_3^=\downarrow$; $Ni^{++} + CO_3^= \rightarrow Ni^{++}CO_3^=$

(continued)

24. $Ca^{++} + 2\ OH^- + 2\ H^+ + 2\ C_2H_3O_2^- \rightarrow Ca^{++} + 2\ C_2H_3O_2^- + 2\ H_2O$; $2\ OH^- + 2\ H^+ \rightarrow 2\ H_2O$
25. $3\ Zn^{++} + 6\ Cl^- + 6\ Na^+ + 2\ PO_4^{\equiv} \rightarrow 6\ Na^+ + 6\ Cl^- + Zn_3^{++}(PO_4)_2^{\equiv}\downarrow$; $3\ Zn^{++} + 2\ PO_4^{\equiv} \rightarrow Zn_3^{++}(PO_4)_2^{\equiv}\downarrow$
26. $3\ Ba^{++} + 3\ CO_3^{=} + 6\ H^+ + 2\ PO_4^{\equiv} \rightarrow Ba_3^{++}(PO_4)_2^{\equiv}\downarrow + 3\ H_2CO_3\ (\rightarrow 3\ H_2O + 3\ CO_2\uparrow)$; same
27. $2\ H^+ + 2\ NO_3^- + Sr^{++} + 2\ OH^- \rightarrow Sr^{++} + 2\ NO_3^- + 2\ H_2O$; $2\ H^+ + 2\ OH^- \rightarrow 2\ H_2O$
28. $2\ H^+ + SO_4^{=} + 2\ Na^+ + 2\ Cl^- \rightleftharpoons 2\ H^+ + 2\ Cl^- + 2\ Na^+ + SO_4^{=}$; NR
29. $2\ K^+ + SO_4^{=} + 2\ NH_4^+ + 2\ NO_3^- \rightleftharpoons 2\ K^+ + 2\ NO_3^- + 2\ NH_4^+ + SO_4^{=}$; NR
30. $Pb^{++} + SO_4^{=} + 2\ Na + 2\ Br^- \rightleftharpoons Pb^{++} + 2\ Br^- + 2\ Na^+ + SO_4^{=}$; NR
31. $Zn^{++} + 2\ ClO_3^- + 2\ NH_4^+ + S^{=} \rightarrow 2\ NH_4^+ + 2\ ClO_3^- + Zn^{++}S^{=}\downarrow$; $Zn^{++} + S^{=} \rightarrow Zn^{++}S^{=}\downarrow$
32. $Ca^{++} + 2\ Cl^- + Mn^{++} + 2\ I^- \rightleftharpoons Ca^{++} + 2\ I^- + Mn^{++} + 2\ Cl^-$; NR
33. $2\ NH_4^+ + SO_4^{=} + Ba^{++} + 2\ OH^- \rightarrow Ba^{++}SO_4^{=}\downarrow + 2\ NH_4OH\ (\rightarrow 2\ NH_3\uparrow + 2\ H_2O)$; same
34. $K^+ + I^- + NH_4^+ + NO_3^- \rightleftharpoons NH_4^+ + I^- + K^+ + NO_3^-$; NR
35. $3\ Hg^{++} + 6\ Cl^- + 2\ Al^{+++} + 6\ Br^- \rightleftharpoons 3\ Hg^{++} + 6\ Br^- + 2\ Al^{+++} + 6\ Cl^-$; NR

Group VI.

1. $NH_4^+ + Cl^- + H_2O \rightleftharpoons NH_4OH\ (\rightarrow NH_3\uparrow + H_2O) + H^+ + Cl^-$
2. $Na^+ + C_2H_3O_2^- + H_2O \rightleftharpoons HC_2H_3O_2 + Na^+ + OH^-$
3. $2\ Li^+ + S^{=} + 2\ H_2O \rightleftharpoons Li^+ + 2\ OH^- + H_2S\uparrow$
4. $2\ NH_4^+ + SO_4^{=} + 2\ H_2O \rightleftharpoons 2\ NH_4OH\ (\rightarrow 2\ NH_3\uparrow + 2\ H_2O) + 2\ H^+ + SO_4^{=}$
5. $K^+ + CN^- + H_2O \rightleftharpoons HCN + K^+ + OH^-$
6. $Rb^+ + C_2H_3O_2^- + H_2O \rightleftharpoons HC_2H_3O_2 + Rb^+ + OH^-$
7. $2\ Na^+ + B_4O_7^{=} + 2\ H_2O \rightleftharpoons H_2B_4O_7 + 2\ Na^+ + 2\ OH^-$
8. $2\ NH_4^+ + S^{=} + 2\ H_2O \rightleftharpoons H_2S\uparrow + 2\ NH_4OH\ (\rightarrow 2\ NH_3\uparrow + 2\ H_2O)$
9. $2\ Li^+ + CO_3^{=} + 2\ H_2O \rightleftharpoons H_2CO_3\ (\rightarrow H_2O + CO_2\uparrow) + 2\ Li^+ + 2\ OH^-$
10. $NH_4^+ + NO_3^- + H_2O \rightleftharpoons NH_4OH\ (\rightarrow NH_3\uparrow + H_2O) + H^+ + NO_3^-$
11. $Ca^{++} + 2\ C_2H_3O_2^- + H_2O \rightleftharpoons 2\ HC_2H_3O_2 + Ca^{++} + 2\ OH^-$
12. $2\ Na^+ + CO_3^{=} + 2\ H_2O \rightleftharpoons H_2CO_3\ (\rightarrow H_2O + CO_2\uparrow) + 2\ Na^+ + 2\ OH^-$
13. $NH_4^+ + C_2H_3O_2^- + H_2O \rightleftharpoons HC_2H_3O_2 + NH_4OH\ (\rightarrow NH_3\uparrow + H_2O)$
14. $2\ K^+ + S^{=} + 2\ H_2O \rightleftharpoons H_2S\uparrow + 2\ K^+ + 2\ OH^-$
15. $NH_4^+ + HCO_3^- + H_2O \rightleftharpoons H_2CO_3\ (\rightarrow H_2O + CO_2\uparrow) + NH_4OH\ (\rightarrow NH_3\uparrow + H_2O)$

Equilibria: pp. 93–97

Group I.

1. $K_{eq} = \dfrac{[SO_3]^2}{[SO_2]^2 \times [O_2]}$
2. $K_{eq} = \dfrac{[CO_2]^2}{[CO]^2 \times [O_2]}$
3. $K_{eq} = \dfrac{[NH_3]^2}{[N_2] \times [H_2]^3}$
4. $K_{eq} = \dfrac{[HCl]^2}{[H_2] \times [Cl_2]}$
5. $K_{eq} = \dfrac{[N_2O]^2}{[N_2]^2 \times [O_2]}$
6. $K_{eq} = \dfrac{[NO_2]^2}{[NO]^2 \times [O_2]}$
7. $K_i = \dfrac{[H^+] \times [C_2H_3O_2^-]}{[HC_2H_3O_2]}$
8. $K_i = \dfrac{[H^+] \times [CN^-]}{[HCN]}$

(continued)

9. $K_{sp} = [Ag^+] \times [Cl^-]$ ([AgCl] = constant)
10. $K_{sp} = [Pb^{2+}] \times [I^-]^2$ ($[PbI_2]$ = constant)
11. $K_{sp} = [Bi^{3+}]^2 \times [S^{2-}]^3$ ($[Bi_2S_3]$ = constant)
12. $K_{sp} = [Ca^{2+}]^3 \times [PO_4^{3-}]^2$ ($[Ca_3(PO_4)_2]$ = constant)

Group II.

1. 4.0
2. 50
3. 0.4
4. 0.045
5. 0.022
6. 0.2
7. 2.67×10^4
8. 0.116
9. 1.0×10^{-5}
10. 2×10^{-7}
11. 1.35×10^{-4}
12. 1.44×10^{-5}
13. 9.12×10^{-14}
14. 6.16×10^{-30}
15. 1.23×10^{-3} mol/L
16. 1.57×10^{-5} g/mL

Group III.

1. $K = \frac{[C]^3 [D]}{[A]^2 [B]} = 1.78$
2. [A] = [B] = 0.071 M
3. K = 0.058 mol/L
4. $K = 1.59 \times 10^{-4}$
5. $[H_2] = 0.10$
6. $[O_2] = 0.5$
7. K = 85.2
8. $K_D = 1$
9. $K_{sp} = 20 \times 10^{-12}$
10. 5×10^{-8} mol/L
11. $K_{sp} = 1.58 \times 10^{-12}$
12. 3×10^{-39} mol/L
13. $K_{sp} = 9.42 \times 10^{-10}$
14. Yes, AgBr will precipitate out ($8.28 \times 10^{-9} > 4.9 \times 10^{-13}$)
15. $[Ca^{2+}] = 7.43 \times 10^{-6}$ M; $[PO_4^{-3}] = 4.95 \times 10^{-6}$ M
16. $[Pb^{2+}] = 1.78 \times 10^{-2}$ mol/L

Le Chatelier's Principal

The effect of (a) increased pressure and (b) increased temperature on each reaction is indicated below by an arrow showing the reaction favored in each case.

Reaction	Increased Pressure	Increased Temperature
1	←	→
2	←	←
3	←	→
4	→	neither
5	→	←
6	neither	→

Acids and Bases: pp. 98–100

1. 10^{-1}, 10^{-13}, 1, 13
2. 1, 10^{-14}, 0, 14
3. 10^{-13}, 10^{-1}, 13, 1
4. 10^{-14}, 1, 14, 0
5. 10^{-3}, 10^{-11}, 3, 11
6. 10^{-3}, 10^{-11}, 3, 11
7. 10^{-3}, 10^{-11}, 3, 11
8. 10^{-11}, 10^{-3}, 11, 3
9. 10^{-10}, 10^{-4}, 10, 4
10. 10^{-10}, 10^{-4}, 10, 4
11. 5×10^{-4}, 2×10^{-11}, 3.3, 10.7
12. 1.5×10^{-4}, 6.7×10^{-11}, 3.8, 10.2
13. 3.5×10^{-6}, 2.9×10^{-9}, 5.5, 8.5
14. 1.8×10^{-4}, 5.5×10^{-11}, 3.7, 10.3
15. 8.7×10^{-5}, 1.1×10^{-10}, 4.1, 9.9
16. 6.7×10^{-7}, 1.5×10^{-8}, 6.2, 7.8
17. 3.2×10^{-8}, 3.1×10^{-7}, 7.5, 6.5
18. 2.7×10^{-6}, 3.8×10^{-9}, 5.6, 8.4
19. 5.0×10^{-5}, 2.0×10^{-10}, 4.3, 9.7
20. 3.5×10^{-6}, 2.8×10^{-9}, 5.5, 8.5
21. 1.3×10^{-12}, 7.7×10^{-3}, 11.9, 2.1
22. 6.4×10^{-12}, 1.6×10^{-3}, 11.2, 2.8
23. 7.9×10^{-11}, 1.3×10^{-4}, 10.1, 3.9
24. 1.2×10^{-12}, 8.4×10^{-3}, 11.9, 2.1
25. $[H^+] = 13.2 \times 10^{-5}$
26. pH = 2.44
27. $K_i = 1.9 \times 10^{-6}$
28. a. 0.50 M CH_3COOH b. $[H^+] = 3.0 \times 10^{-3}$
29. $[H^+] = [ClO^-] = 4.10 \times 10^{-5}$ M
30. pH = 3.0
31. pH = 9.05
32. a. $HF(aq) + CH_3COO^-(aq) \rightarrow F^-(aq) + CH_3COOH(aq)$
    b. $H_2S(aq) + CO_3^{-2}(aq) \rightarrow HS^- + HCO_3^-(aq)$
    c. $NH_4^+(aq) + F^-(aq) \rightarrow HF(aq) + NH_3(aq)$
33. a. $K_a = \dfrac{[NO_2^-]\,[NH_4^+]}{[HNO_2]\,[NH_3]}$ b. $K_a = \dfrac{[C_6H_5COO^-]\,[CH_3COOH]}{[C_6H_5COOH]\,[CH_3COO^-]}$

(continued)

34. a. HSO_4^- and SO_4^{2-} ; $C_2O_4^{2-}$ and $HC_2O_2^-$; b. $H_2PO_4^-$ and HPO_4^{2-} ; HCO_3^- and H_2CO_3 ; c. H_2O and OH^- ; S^{2-} and HS^- ; d. HCN and CN^- ; $HC_2H_3O_2$ and $C_2H_3O_2^-$; e. HNO_2 and NO_2^- ; H_3O^+ H_2O.

35. a. base; b. base; c. base; d. acid; e. acid; f. acid; g. base; h. acid

Standard Solutions: pp. 101–113

- EQUIVALENT WEIGHT

Group I.

1. 8.00; 0.00800
2. 6.01; 0.00601; 4.00; 0.00400; 3.00; 0.00300
3. 36.30; 0.03630; 18.15; 0.01815
4. 60.32; 0.06032; 45.24; 0.04524; 36.19; 0.03619
5. 53.20; 0.05320; 35.47; 0.03547; 26.60; 0.02660
6. 19.00; 0.01900
7. 44.44; 0.04444
8. 195.57; 0.19557
9. 42.00; 0.04200
10. 23.95; 0.02395
11. 82.05; 0.08205
12. 66.08; 0.06608
13. 49.04; 0.04904; 98.08; 0.09808
14. 70.76; 0.07076
15. 98.52; 0.09852
16. 64.06; 0.06406
17. 122.55; 0.12255
18. 102.42; 0.10242
19. 162.31; 0.16231
20. 32.67; 0.03267; 49.00; 0.04900; 98.00; 0.09800
21. 126.53; 0.12653
22. 79.07; 0.07907
23. 37.05; 0.03705
24. 168.36; 0.16836
25. 159.59; 0.15959

Group II.

1. 1.00
2. 1.00
3. 2.000
4. 2.0
5. 1.00
6. 4.00 or 2.00
7. 0.33
8. 3.000
9. 0.840
10. 0.72
11. 2.81
12. 2.78
13. 6.36
14. 1.06
15. 1.39
16. 7.45
17. 0.926
18. 0.117
19. 0.164
20. 1.08

• STANDARD SOLUTIONS

Group III.

1. 74.6 g in 1 L
2. 211.6 g in 1 L
3. 142 g in 1 L
4. 173.7 g in 2 L
5. 1065 g in 5 L
6. 11.1 g in 1 L
7. 13.3 g in 1 L
8. 17 g in 1 L
9. 0.58 g in 1 L
10. 4.8 g in 500 mL
11. 8.36 g in 40 mL
12. 4.68 g in 600 mL
13. 6.84 g in 100 mL
14. 0.54 g in 250 mL
15. 53 g in 50 mL
16. 10.45 g in 400 mL
17. 492 g in 500 mL
18. 1.95 g in 25 mL
19. 18.37 g in 100 mL
20. 738 g in 750 mL
21. 36.5 g in 1 L
22. 147 g in 1 L
23. 44.4 g in 1 L
24. 32.7 g or 49.0 g or 98.0 g in 1 L
25. 255 g
26. 80. g in 1 L
27. 129.6 g in 1 L
28. 284 g in 1 L
29. 378 g in 1 L
30. 6.8 g in 1 L
31. 8.6 g in 1 L
32. 10.42 g in 1 L
33. 8.1 g in 1 L
34. 22.3 g in 1 L
35. 14.8 g in 1 L
36. 1.025 g in 1 L
37. 0.91 g in 1 L
38. 0.608 g in 1 L
39. 2.99 g in 1 L
40. 6.8 g in 1 L
41. 114 g in 2 L
42. 375.1 g in 4 L
43. 64 g in 500 mL
44. 12.7 g in 200 mL
45. 42 g in 750 mL
46. 13.57 g in 100 mL
47. 69.8 g in 250 mL
48. 1.47 g in 300 mL
49. 2.77 g in 500 mL
50. 0.774 g in 100 mL
51. 1.75 g in 250 mL
52. 16.1 g in 50 mL
53. 2.72 g in 25 mL
54. 0.049 g in 30 mL
55. 2.40 g in 200 mL
56. 0.50 g in 350 mL
57. 0.239 g in 150 mL
58. 13.1 g in 50 mL
59. 3.8 g in 250 mL
60. 94.57 g in 8 L

Group IV.

1. 1.0; 1.0
2. 1.000; 1.000
3. 1.000; 3.000
4. 1.000; 2.000
5. 1.00; 6.00
6. 1.00; 1.00
7. 2.00; 4.00
8. 0.125; 0.125
9. 0.28; 0.28
10. 1.33; 4.00
11. 0.25; 0.25
12. 0.50; 0.50
13. 0.324; 0.648
14. 0.635; 0.635
15. 0.900; 5.40
16. 0.044; 0.044
17. 0.11; 0.22
18. 0.324; 0.972
19. 0.77; 1.5
20. 0.557; 1.11
21. 0.0085; 0.017
22. 0.77; 0.77
23. 0.62; 0.62
24. 0.026; 0.17
25. 0.087; 0.17

- PERCENT SOLUTIONS

Group V.

1. 5.0% (w/v)
2. 2.5% (w/w)
3. 1.0% (v/v)
4. 6.0% (w/v)
5. 1.0% (w/v)
6. 3.0% (w/w)
7. 7.5% (v/v)
8. 6.3% (w/v)
9. 1.38% (w/w)
10. 0.577% (v/v)
11. 3.2% (w/v)
12. 0.217% (w/w)

Group VI.

1. 1.5 g
2. 2.3 g
3. 1.3 g
4. 0.063 g
5. 0.90 g
6. 1.4 g
7. 0.59 g
8. 2.0 g
9. 0.79 g
10. 0.050 g
11. 0.0048 g
12. 1.02 g

Group VII.

1. 100 mL
2. 200 mL
3. 50 mL
4. 300 mL
5. 12.5 mL
6. 111.1 mL
7. 560 mL
8. 130 mL
9. 400 mL
10. 230 mL
11. 560 mL
12. 320 mL

Group VIII.

1. 12
2. 15.6
3. 36.1
4. 15
5. 17.6
6. 2.7
7. 8
8. 5.3
9. 5.30
10. 20

Group IX.

Dilute each of the given solutions with distilled water as follows:

1. to 1.0 L
2. to 6.0 L
3. to 5.0 L
4. to 2.0 L
5. to 2.4 L
6. to 3.0 L
7. to 10 L
8. to $5\bar{0}0$ mL
9. to $4\bar{0}0$ mL
10. to 1.0 L

Group X.

Dilute each of the given solutions with distilled water as follows:

1. to 5.0 L
2. to $2\bar{0}0$ L
3. to 1800 L
4. to $3\bar{0}0$ L
5. to $5\bar{0}0$ mL
6. to 25 L
7. to 1.0 L
8. to $2\bar{0}0$ L
9. to 10. L
10. to 40. L

• TITRATIONS

Group XI.

1. a. 20. mL
   b. 4$\bar{0}$0 mL
   c. 1.0 mL
   d. 0.80 mL
   e. 2.0 L
   f. 4.0 mL
   g. 10. mL
   h. 2.0 mL
   i. 40. mL
   j. 8.0 mL
2. a. 1.0 N
   b. 0.040 N
   c. 2.0 N
   d. 0.10 N
   e. 0.25 N
   f. 0.14 N
   g. 0.50 N
   h. 0.16 N
   i. 0.80 N
   j. 0.33 N
3. 40. mL
4. 0.48 N
5. 0.29 N
6. 4.5 mL
7. 6.0 mL
8. 1.3 N
9. 0.0077 N
10. 79 mL
11. a. 1250 mL
    b. 27 mL
    c. 2200 mL
    d. 830 mL
    e. 1.2 mL
    f. 7500 mL
    g. 1100 mL
    h. 1800 mL
    i. 270 mL
    j. 61 mL
12. 0.482 N
13. 0.662 N
14. 270 mL
15. 0.49 N
16. a. 0.946 N
    b. 0.289 N
    c. 0.342 N
    d. 0.122 N
    e. 0.899 N
    f. 0.218 N
    g. 0.520 N
    h. 0.351 N
    i. 0.462 N
    j. 0.458 N
    k. 0.295 N
    l. 0.0299 N

• MOLAL SOLUTIONS

1. a. Dissolve 58.5 g of NaCl in 1.0 kg of water.
   b. Dissolve 200 g (196 g) of H_2SO_4 in 1 kg of water.
   c. Dissolve 86 g of sucrose in 1 kg of water.
   d. Dissolve 23 g of ethyl alcohol in 500 g of water.
   e. Dissolve 24.5 g of H_3PO_4 in 500 g of water.
   f. Dissolve 24 g of HNO_3 in 1.5 kg of water.
   g. Dissolve 0.90 g of NaOH in 75 g of water.
   h. Dissolve 2.62 g of NH_4OH in 150 g of water.
2. a. 1.00 m; b. 0.250 m; c. 0.342 m; d. 0.702 m; e. 0.17 m; f. 0.12 m; g. 1.22 m; h. 1.2 m

Colligative Properties: pp. 114–115

1. 100.52° C
2. −0.93° C
3. 100.13° C
4. −0.74° C
5. 100.15° C
6. −0.640° C
7. 2.66° C
8. 2.43° C
9. 40
10. 35
11. 62.6
12. 140
13. 58.5
14. 112.6
15. 37.5 g

(continued)

Redox Reactions: pp. 116–121

Given below are the coefficients that the equations will have when properly balanced. They are given in the same order as that found in the original problem.

1. 1-1-1-1-2
2. 2-1-2-1
3. 1-2-1-2-1
4. 1-1-2-1-2-1
5. 1-6-3-1-3-3
6. 2-4-2-2-1
7. 1-2-1-2-1
8. 1-2-1-2
9. 1-1-2-2
10. 4-1-4-1
11. 10-2-48-15-1-2-48
12. 2-2-3-2-4
13. 3-4-3-1-2
14. 3-8-6-2-3-4
15. 1-4-1-1-1-2
16. 3-3-2-1-3
17. 6-6-5-1-6
18. 1-2-2-1-1-2
19. 1-2-1-2
20. 1-9-9-1-3-9
21. 1-10-10-2-2-10-7
22. 3-3-1-3-1-2
23. 2-16-2-2-3-8
24. 1-8-3-2-2-3-7
25. 4-4-1-1-4-2-2
26. 3-6-2-3-3-2-4
27. 1-2-7-2-2-5
28. 3-4-2-1-4-2
29. 2-5-6-2-2-5-3
30. 1-4-1-1-2-2-2
31. 1-2-1-1-1-2
32. 2-5-3-2-5-4
33. 2-5-26-2-15-12
34. 4-8-4-6-5
35. 3-6-4-4-3-6-4
36. 1-2-2-1-1
37. 3-5-3-5-1-5
38. 3-5-1-3-3-3-3
39. 5-2-2-2-2-5-2
40. 3-12-14-6-6-14-10
41. 1-1-1-1-1
42. 2-16-5-2-5-5-7
43. 2-15-1-4-11
44. 1-2-1-1-1
45. 6-5-2-10-6-5-2-2-1
46. 3-5-1-3-3-6-3
47. 1-2-2-1-2-1-1
48. 1-10-12-1-10-6-6
49. 1-1-2-1-2-1
50. 1-2-2-1-2-1-1
51. 3-4-1-3-4
52. 4-5-12-4-8-5-6
53. 2-1-1-1-2
54. 3-30-10-6-15-10-20
55. 2-16-2-2-5-8
56. 3-5-2-2-5
57. 3-10-4-6-15-10
58. 1-6-2-2-3
59. 1-1-2-1-1-1
60. 2-3-3-1-3-3
61. 1-3-1-3
62. 1-1-1-1
63. 15-20-4-12-3-12-12
64. 2-4-1-2-2
65. 2-4-4-2-4-1-2
66. 1-4-6-6-1-2-3
67. 1-1-2-1-2
68. 1-5-6-6-3-3
69. 6-1-1-3-3
70. 1-1-14-6-2-2-7
71. 5-4-24-10-2-4-9
72. 1-6-1-6
73. 5-6-16-10-6-3-6
74. 1-2-2-2-4
75. 6-1-5-6-3-3
76. 1-5-1-3-2-3-3
77. 1-2-2-1-1-1
78. 2-3-3-2-4
79. 5-2-6-10-2-2-8
80. 2-1-6-1-5-3
81. 3-1-3-3-1
82. 1-6-2-1-3
83. 6-16-6-3-4-8
84. 3-8-3-2-3-4

Nuclear Chemistry: pp. 122–126

Group I.

1. ${}^{1}_{0}n$
2. ${}^{63}_{30}Zn$
3. ${}^{1}_{0}n$
4. ${}^{1}_{0}n$
5. ${}^{1}_{1}H$
6. ${}^{2}_{1}H$
7. ${}^{1}_{0}n$
8. ${}^{3}_{1}H$
9. ${}^{1}_{0}n$
10. ${}^{1}_{0}n$
11. γ
12. α
13. α
14. ${}^{242}_{96}Cm$
15. ${}^{25}_{13}Al$
16. ${}^{1}_{1}H$
17. ${}^{139}_{57}La$
18. ${}^{1}_{0}n$
19. ${}^{0}_{-1}e$
20. ${}^{3}_{1}H$
21. γ
22. ${}^{214}_{83}Bi$
23. ${}^{62}_{29}Cu$
24. ${}^{1}_{0}n$
25. ${}^{3}_{2}He$
26. ${}^{241}_{95}Am$
27. ${}^{1}_{0}n$
28. ${}^{1}_{1}H$
29. ${}^{1}_{1}H$
30. γ
31. α
32. ${}^{1}_{1}H$
33. α
34. ${}^{30}_{15}P$
35. $X = \alpha$

Group II.

Missing member only is shown.

1. $^{7}_{4}Be$
2. $^{14}_{6}C$
3. $^{1}_{1}H$
4. $^{1}_{1}H$
5. $^{13}_{7}N$
6. $^{125}_{53}I$
7. α
8. $^{30}_{15}P$
9. $^{27}_{12}Mg$
10. $^{7}_{4}Be$

Group III.

Various methods are possible in each case. Only one possible method is shown here.

1. $^{152}Sm(d, \gamma)^{154}Eu$
2. $^{19}F(p,d)^{18}F$
3. $^{45}Sc(n, \gamma)^{46}Sc$
4. $^{93}Nb(\alpha, \gamma)^{97}Tc$
5. $^{94}Zr(p, \gamma)^{95}Nb$
6. $^{84}Kr(d,p)^{85}Kr$
7. $^{142}Ce(p,n)^{142}Pr$
8. $^{88}Sr(d, \gamma)^{90}Y$
9. $^{100}Ru(\alpha,n)^{103}Pd$
10. $^{195}Pt(\alpha,e^{+})^{199}Au$

Group IV.

1. 4.0 g
2. 2.0 g
3. 4.0 g
4. 1.56 g
5. 1.88 g
6. 1.72×10^{7} y
7. 40.8 d
8. 13,950 y
9. 16.0 g
10. 80. g
11. 3.0 m
12. 2.5 d

Organic Chemistry: pp. 127–146

Group I.

1. alkane (none)
2. alcohol (–OH)
3. aldehyde (–CHO)
4. alkane (none)
5. aldehyde (–CHO)
6. ether (–O–)
7. ketone (–C=O) (with a single bond line below the C)
8. alkene (–C=C–) (with a single bond line below each C)
9. alkyl halide (halogenated hydrocarbon) (–X)
10. carboxylic acid (–COOH)
11. ketone (–C=O)
12. carboxylic acid (–COOH)
13. alkyne (–C≡C–)
14. amine ($-NH_2$)
15. alkyl halide or halogenated hydrocarbon (–X)

Group II.

1. n-hexane
2. 3-methylheptane
3. 2,4-dimethylhexane
4. 4-ethylheptane
5. 3-ethyl-2,3-dimethylhexane
6. n-butane
7. 3-ethylpentane
8. 5-ethyl-2-methylheptane
9. 2,3,4-trimethylheptane
10. 2-bromo-4-methylhexane
11. 5-ethyl-3,4-dimethylheptane
12. 2,3-dichloro-3-ethyl-5-methylhexane
13. 4,5-diethyl-4-methyloctane
14. 5,6-dichloro-2-methylnonane
15. 2,7-dibromo-1-chloro-4-methyloctane
16. 7-chloro-5-ethyl-2-methyl-4-propyloctane
17. 3-bromo-5-ethylnonane
18. 1-4-6-triiodooctane
19. 6-fluoro-3-iodo-4-methyloctane
20. 4-ethyl-6-iodo-2-methylnonane
21. ethene
22. 3-heptene
23. 2,3-dimethyl-3-hexene
24. 5-chloro-4-methyl-1-hexene
25. 6-bromo-4-methyl-2-octene
26. 5,6-dimethyl-2-heptene
27. 7-chloro-4-ethyl-2-methyl-3-heptene
28. 6,7-dichloro-3-methyl-2-heptene

(continued)

29. 6-chloro-3-octene
30. 6-chloro-4,4,7,7-tetramethyl-2-nonene
31. 7-bromo-5,5-dichloro-2-heptene
32. 4-ethyl-3-heptene
33. 2,4-dibromo-6-methyl-3-heptene
34. 5,7-dibromo-4-methyl-3-heptene
35. 5-bromo-7,8-dichloro-3-octene
36. propyne
37. 2-butyne
38. 1-bromo-2-pentyne
39. 5-methyl-2-hexyne
40. 2-bromo-3-methyl-4-octyne
41. 1-butanol
42. 1-propanol
43. 2-pentanol
44. 2-butanol
45. 4-heptanol
46. 2-heptanol
47. 2-chloro-3-pentanol
48. 2-methyl-1-butanol
49. 3-methyl-2-pentanol
50. 3,5-dimethyl-2-hexanol
51. 2,2,6-trimethyl-4-heptanol
52. 4-chloro-5-methyl-1-hexanol
53. 1,2-dichloro-4-methyl-3-pentanol
54. 2,3-dimethyl-4-heptanol
55. 1,3-dichloro-2-butanol
56. 5,5-diethyl-2-heptanol
57. 6-bromo-4,7-dichloro-2-heptanol
58. 3-ethyl-2-methyl-1-hexanol
59. 1,4-butanediol
60. 1,4-hexanediol
61. ethanal
62. 3-hexanone
63. butanal
64. 3-methylbutanal
65. 3,3-dimethylpentanal
66. 3-chloropentanal
67. 2,4,4-trimethylpentanal
68. 4,4-dimethylpentanal
69. 3-octanone
70. 2-methyl-4-heptanone
71. 5,5-dimethyl-3-hexanone
72. 3,6-dichloroheptanal
73. 5-iodo-7-methyl-2-octanone
74. 2,5-diiodohexanal
75. 4-iodo-6,6-dimethyl-3-heptanone
76. 1-bromo-7-methyl-4-octanone
77. 5,5,7-trichloro-3-heptanone
78. 3-methylhexanal
79. 1-chloro-7,7-dimethyl-4-octanone
80. 3,3-dimethyl-5-chloroheptanal
81. dimethyl ether
82. methylethyl ether
83. methyl-n-propyl ether
84. methyl-n-pentyl ether
85. ethyl-t-butyl ether
86. butanoic acid
87. pentanoic acid
88. 2,2-dimethylbutanoic acid
89. 3-methylbutanoic acid
90. butanedioic acid
91. 4-methylhexanoic acid
92. 2,4-dimethylpentanoic acid
93. 3-chlorohexanoic acid
94. 4-fluorohexanoic acid
95. 2-aminobutanoic acid
96. 2-bromobutanoic acid
97. 2,4-dibromopentanoic acid
98. 2-aminopentanoic acid
99. 3-hydroxybutanoic acid
100. 2-hydroxyhexanoic acid

Group III.

1. $CH_3CH_2CH_2CH_3$
2. $CH_3CHClCH_2CH_2CH_3$
3. $CH_3CH_2CH(CH_3)CH_2CH_2CH_3$
4. $CH_3(CH_2)_5CH_3$
5. $CH_3C(CH_3)_2CH_2CH(CH_3)CH_2CH_2CH_3$
6. $CH_3CH(CH_3)CH(CH_3)CHCl(CH_2)_3CH_3$
7. $CH_2ClCHClCH_2CHClCH_3$
8. $CH_3CH(CH_3)CH(CH_3)CH(CH_3)CH_2CH_3$

(continued)

9. $CH_3CH(CH_3)C(CH_3)_2CH_2CH_2CH_2CH_3$
10. $CH_3CH(CH_3)CH_2CClBr(CH_2)_5CH_3$
11. $CH_3CH(CH_3)C(CH_3) = CHCH_2CH_3$
12. $CH_2 = CClCH_2CH_2CH_3$
13. $CH_3CH_2CH = CH(CH_2)_3CH_3$
14. $CH_3CH(CH_3)C(CH_3) = C(C_2H_5)\,(CH_2)_4CH_3$
15. $CH_3C(CH_3)_2C(CH_3) = CHCH(CH_3)$
 $CH_2CH_2CH_3$
16. $CH_2BrCCl_2CH = CBrCHBrCH_2CH_3$
17. $CH_2 = CFCClFCH_3$
18. $CH_2 = CHCH = CH_2$
19. CH_3CH_2OH
20. $CH_3CHOHCH_3$
21. $CH_3CHOHCH_2CH_2CH_3$
22. $CH_3CHOHC(CH_3)_2CH_2CH_2CH_3$
23. $CHClOHCHClCHClCH_3$
24. $CH_2OHC(CH_3)_2CH(C_2H_5)CH_2CH_2CH_3$
25. $CH_3C(CH_3)\,(OH)CH_2C(CH_3)_2CH_2CH_2CH_3$
26. $CHClOHCHBrCHClC(CH_3)_2$
 $CH_2CHClCHClCH_2CH_2CH_3$
27. $CH_2OHCH_2CHOHCH_3$
28. $CH_3CBr_2C(CH_3)\,(OH)CH(CH_3)CH_2CH_3$
29. $CH_2FC(CH_3)_2C(OH)\,(CH_3)CHFCH_2CH_2CH_3$
30. $CHOHCl(CH_3)CH(C_2H_5)Cl(CH_3)$
 $CH(CH_3)\,(CH_2)_3CH_3$
31. $CH_3(CH_2)_5CHO$
32. $CH_3CH_2CH_2CHO$
33. $CH_3\overset{*}{C}OCH_2CH_2CH_3$
34. $(C_2H_5)_2\overset{*}{C}O$
35. $CH_3CH_2CH_2\overset{*}{C}OCH_2CH_2CH_2CH_2CH_3$
36. $CH_3CH_2CH_2CH(C_2H_5)CH(CH_3)CHO$
37. $CH_3CHBrCCl_2CHO$
38. $CH_3CCl(CH_3)\overset{*}{C}OCH(CH_3)CH_2CH_3$
39. CH_2O
40. $CH_3CH_2C(CH_3)_2CH(CH_3)CHO$
41. $CH_3CH(CH_3)\overset{*}{C}OC(CH_3)_2CH_2CH_2CH_3$
42. $CH_3\overset{*}{C}OC(CH_3)_2CClICH_3$
43. $CH_3CH_2CH_2CHClCHClCH_2$
 $CHClCHBrCHBrCHO$
44. $CH_3CH(CH_3)CH(CH_3)\overset{*}{C}OC(CH_3)\,(C_2H_5)$
 $CH_2CH(C_2H_5)CH_2CH_3$
45. $CH_3CH_2CH_2COOH$
46. $HOOCCH_2CH_2CH_2COOH$
47. $CH_3CH(NH_2)COOH$
48. $CH_3CHClCHClCOOH$
49. $CH_3CH_2CH_2C(CH_3)_2CH_2COOH$
50. $CH_3CHOHCH_2CH_2COOH$
51. $CH_3(CH_2)_5CHBrCHBrCHBrCOOH$
52. $CH_3CHICl_2CH_2CH(CH_3)COOH$
53. $CH_3CH_2CHOHCOOH$
54. $HOOCCH_2CH_2COOH$
55. $CH_3CH_2CHOHCH_2COOH$
56. $CH_3CH_2CHClCH(CH_3)CH(CH_3)COOH$
57. $CH_3CH_2CH_2CHClCH_2$
 $CHClCHBrCHBrCHClCOOH$
58. $CH_3CH_2C(NH_2)_2COOH$
59. $CH_3CH_2CHClCHClCH_2CH_2CH_2COOH$
60. $CH_3CHOHCH_2CHOHCOOH$

*indicates a ketone group, not an ether linkage

Group IV.

1. $CH_4 + Cl_2 \rightarrow CH_3Cl(+Cl_2) \rightarrow CH_2Cl_2(+Cl_2) \rightarrow CHCl_3(+Cl_2) \rightarrow CCl_4$
2. $CH_3CH = CH_2 + Cl_2 \rightarrow CH_3CHClCH_2Cl$
3. $CH_2 = CH_2$ (polymerized) $\rightarrow$ (step 1) $CH_3CH_2CH = CH_2 \rightarrow$ (further steps) $CH_3(CH_2)_nCH = CH_2$
4. $C_2H_5Cl + NaOH \rightarrow NaCl + C_2H_5OH$
5. $CH_3(CH_2)_4CHO + H_2 \rightarrow CH_3(CH_2)_4CH_2OH$

(continued)

6. $C_2H_6 + Br_2 \rightarrow C_2H_5Br + HBr$
7. $CH_3CH_2CH = CHCH_2CH_3 + HCl \rightarrow CH_3CH_2CH_2CHClCH_2CH_3$
8. $CH_3CH = CHCH_3 + H_2 \rightarrow CH_3CH_2CH_2CH_3$
9. $(C_{17}H_{35}COO)_3C_3H_5 + 3HOH \rightarrow 3C_{17}H_{35}COOH + C_3H_5(OH)_3$
10. $C_6H_6 + Cl_2 \rightarrow C_6H_5Cl + HCl$
11. $CH_3CHOHCH_2CH_3 + H_2SO_4 \rightarrow CH_3CH(OSO_3H)CH_2CH_3 + H_2O$
12. $2\,C_8H_{18} + 25\,O_2 \rightarrow 16\,CO_2 + 18\,H_2O$
13. $CH_3\overset{O}{\overset{\|}{C}}\,CH_2CH_2CH_3 + HCN \rightarrow CH_3C(OH)(CN)CH_2CH_2CH_3$
14. $2CH_2OHCH_2CH_2CH_3 + 2Na — 2CH_2ONaCH_2CH_2CH_3 + H_2$
15. $CH_3CH_2CH_2CH_3 + Br_2 \rightarrow$ mixture of $CH_2BrCH_2CH_2CH_3 + CH_3CHBrCH_2CH_3$
16. $CH \equiv CH + HCl \rightarrow CH_2 = CHCl$
17. $CH_2 = CHCH_2CH_3 + Cl_2 \rightarrow CH_2ClCHClCH_2CH_3$
18. $CH_3CH = CH_2$ (polymerized) → (first step)

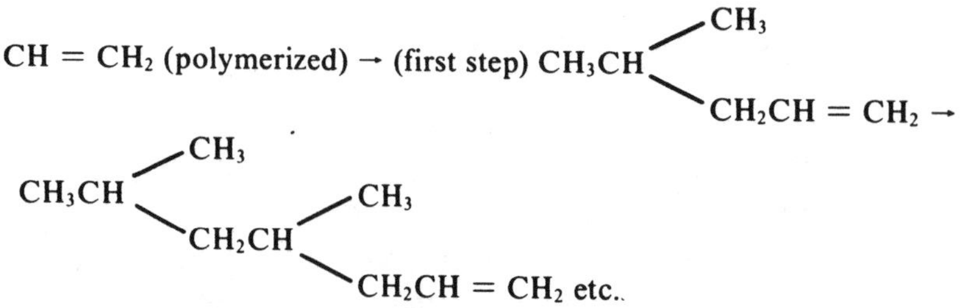

19. $C_6H_6 + Br_2 \rightarrow C_6H_5Br(+Br_2) \rightarrow C_6H_4Br_2$ (mixture of ortho and para forms)
20. $HCOOH + CH_3CH_2CHOHCH_2CH_2CH_3 — CH_3CH_2CH(OOCH)CH_2CH_2CH_3 + H_2O$
21. $3CH_3CH_2CH_2OH + PCl_3 \rightarrow P(OH)_3 + 3CH_3CH_2CH_2Cl$
22. $CH_2 = CHCH_2CH_2CH_3 + HBr \rightarrow CH_3CHBrCH_2CH_2CH_3$
23. $2\,C_{12}H_{26} + 37\,O_2 \rightarrow 24\,CO_2 + 26\,H_2O$
24. $C_6H_5CH_3 + Br_2 \rightarrow C_6H_5CH_2Br(\text{or } C_6H_4ClCH_3) + HBr$
25. $CH_3CH = CH(CH_2)_4CH_3 + CH_3CH_2CH_2CH_3 \rightarrow CH_3CH_2CH(CH_2CH_2CH_2CH_3)(CH_2)_4CH_3$
26. $CH_3CH_2CH_3 + Cl_2 \rightarrow$ mixture of $CH_2ClCH_2CH_3$ and $CH_3CHClCH_3$
27. $CH_2 = CHCH_2CH_3 + H_2 \rightarrow CH_3CH_2CH_2CH_3$
28. $CH_3CHOH(CH_2)_5CH_3 + HNO_3 \rightarrow CH_3CH(ONO_2)(CH_2)_5CH_3 + H_2O$
29. $CH_3CH = CHCH_2CH_3 + HCN \rightarrow$ mixture of $CH_3CH_2CH(CN)CH_2CH_3$ and $CH_3CHCNCH_2CH_2CH_3$
30. $CH_3CHOHCH_2CH_3 + (O) \rightarrow CH_3\overset{O}{\overset{\|}{C}}CH_2CH_3 + H_2O$
31. $CH_3CH_2CH = CH_2$ (polymerized) → (step 1) $CH_3CH_2CH(CH_2CH_2CH = CH_2)CH_3$, etc.
32. $CH \equiv CCH_3 + Br_2 \rightarrow CHBr = CBrCH_3$
33. $CH_3CH_2CH_2CH_2CH_3 + Br_2 \rightarrow$ 1,2, or 3 monobromopentane + HBr
34. $2CH_3CHOHCH_2CH_2CH_3 + 2Na \rightarrow 2CH_3CHONaCH_2CH_2CH_3 + H_2$
35. $CH_3CH = CHCH_2CH_2CH_3 + CH_3CH_2CH_3 \rightarrow$ mixture of $CH_3CH_2CH(CH_2CH_2CH_3)CH_2CH_2CH_3$ and $CH_3CH(CH_2CH_2CH_3)CH_2CH_2CH_2CH_3$
36. $CH_3CHOHCH_3 + CH_3CH_2CH_2COOH \rightarrow CH_3CH(OOCCH_2CH_2CH_3)CH_3 + H_2O$
37. $CH_3CH = CHCH_2CH_3 + Br_2 \rightarrow CH_3CHBrCHBrCH_2CH_3$
38. $3CH_3CH_2CHOHCH_2CH_2CH_3 + PCl_3 \rightarrow 3CH_3CH_2CHClCH_2CH_2CH_3 + P(OH)_3$

(continued)

39. $2\ C_{18}CH_{38} + 55\ O_2 \rightarrow 36\ CO_2 + 38\ H_2O$
40. $CH_2 = CHCH_2CH_3 + CH_3CH_3 \rightarrow CH_3CH(CH_2CH_3)CH_2CH_3$
41. $CH_3CH_2CH_2CH_2COOH + CH_3CH_2CH_2CH_2OH \rightarrow CH_3CH_2CH_2CH_2COOCH_2CH_2CH_2CH_3 + H_2O$
42. $CH_3CH_2\overset{\overset{O}{\|}}{C}\ CH_2CH_2CH_3 + HCN \rightarrow CH_3CH_2C(OH)\ (CN)CH_2CH_2CH_3$
43. $CH_3CH_2CHOHCH_2CH_2CH_3 + (O) \rightarrow CH_3CH_2\overset{\overset{O}{\|}}{C}\ CH_2CH_2CH_3$
44. $(C_{15}H_{31}COO)\ (C_{17}H_{35}COO)_2C_3H_5 + 3HOH \rightarrow C_3H_5(OH)_3 + C_{15}H_{31}COOH + 2C_{17}H_{35}COOH$
45. $CH_3CH_2OH + CH_3COOH \rightarrow CH_3COOCH_2CH_3 + H_2O$
46. $CH_3CH(NH_2)COOH$ (polymerized) $\rightarrow CH_3CH(NH_2)\overset{\overset{O}{/\!/}}{C} - NH - CH(CH_3)COOH$, etc.
47. $(C_{11}H_{23}COO)_3C_3H_5 + 3HOH \rightarrow C_3H_5(OH)_3 + 3C_{11}H_{23}COOH$
48. $2CH_3CH_2OH + 2K \rightarrow 2CH_3CH_2OK + H_2$
49. $CH_3CHOHCH_2CH_3 + CH_3CH_2COOH \rightarrow CH_3CH(OOCCH_2CH_3)CH_2CH_3 + H_2O$
50. $CH \equiv CCH_2CH_3 + HCN \rightarrow CH_2 = C(CN)CH_2CH_3$
51. $C_6H_6 + 3Cl_2$ (in 6 steps, with ultraviolet light as a catalyst) $\rightarrow C_6H_6Cl_6$ (hexachlorocyclohexane). This reaction proceeds with difficulty beyond the second step.
52. $CH_2(NH_2)COOH$ (polymerized) $\rightarrow CH_2(NH_2)\overset{\overset{O}{/\!/}}{C} - NH - CH_2COOH$, etc.
53. $CH_3CH(CH_3)CH_2CH_3 + Br_2 \rightarrow$ mixture of isomeric monobromopentanes
54. $CH_3CH(NH_2)COOH + CH_2(NH_2)COOH \rightarrow CH_3CH(NH_2)\overset{\overset{O}{/\!/}}{C} - NH - CH_2COOH$ (or reverse sequence)
55. $CH_3CHOHCH_2CH_2CH_2CH_3 + HCl \rightarrow CH_3CHClCH_2CH_2CH_2CH_3 + H_2O$
56. $CH_3CH_2CH_2CHO + HCN \rightarrow CH_3CH_2CH_2\underset{\underset{CN}{|}}{CHOH}$
57. $C_6H_5CH_3 + HNO_3 \rightarrow C_6H_4(NO_2)CH_3$ (mixture of ortho and para isomers)
58. $CH_3CH_2CH_2COOH + CH_3CH_2CH_2CH_2OH \rightarrow CH_3CH_2CH_2COOCH_2CH_2CH_2CH_3 + H_2O$
59. $CH_3(CH_2)_4CHO + (O) \rightarrow CH_3(CH_2)_4COOH$
60. $CH_2 = C(CH_3)CH_2CH_2CH_3 + Br_2 \rightarrow CH_2BrCBr(CH_3)CH_2CH_2CH_3$
61. $C_6H_5OH + NaOH \rightarrow C_6H_5ONa + H_2O$
62. $CH_2O + NH_3 \rightarrow \underset{\underset{NH_2}{|}}{H_2COH}$
63. $C_3H_5(OH)_3 + 3CH_3CH_2CH_2COOH \rightarrow C_3H_5(OOCCH_2CH_2CH_3)_3 + 3H_2O$
64. $2C_6H_5OH + CH_2O \rightarrow (- C_6H_4OH - CH_2 - C_6H_4OH - CH_2 -)x$
65. $CH_3CH_2CH_2CH_2CHO + HCl \rightarrow CH_3CH_2CH_2CH_2CHCl(OH)$
66. $CH_3CH = CHCH_2CH_2CH_3 + HCl \rightarrow CH_3CH_2CHClCH_2CH_2CH_3$ and $CH_3CHClCH_2CH_2CH_2CH_3$
67. $C_6H_6 + H_2SO_4 \rightarrow C_6H_5SO_3H + H_2O$
68. $3(CH_3)_3COH + PCl_3 \rightarrow 3(CH_3)_3CCl + P(OH)_3$

(continued)

69. $CH_3CH_2\overset{\overset{O}{\|}}{C}\ CH_2CH_3 + H_2 \rightarrow CH_3CH_2CHOHCH_2CH_3$
70. $2CH_3OH + 2K \rightarrow 2CH_3OK + H_2$
71. $CH_3CH_2CHO + H_2 \rightarrow CH_3CH_2CH_2OH$
72. $CH_3(CH_2)_4CH_3 + Br_2 \rightarrow$ mixture of 1, 2, 3 monobromohexanes
73. $C_6H_6 + HNO_3 \rightarrow C_6H_5NO_2(+HNO_3)\ \ C_6H_4(NO_2)_2$ (meta form)
74. $CH_3CH_2CH_2CHO + (O) \rightarrow CH_3CH_2CH_2COOH$
75. $CH_3(CH_2)_6CH_3 + F_2 \rightarrow$ mixture of 1, 2, 3, 4 monofluorooctanes

Quantum Mechanics: pp. 147–148

Group I.

1. 6.00×10^{14} Hz; 3.98×10^{-19} J
2. 5.0×10^{-7} m; 3.98×10^{-19} J
3. 6.8×10^{14} Hz; 4.4×10^{-7} m
4. 3.53×10^{14} Hz; 2.34×10^{-19} J
5. 6.7×10^{-6} m; 3.0×10^{-20} J
6. 1.30×10^{16} Hz; 2.31×10^{-8} m
7. 2.4×10^{14} Hz; 1.59×10^{-19} J
8. 3.65×10^{-8} m; 5.45×10^{-18} J
9. 1.84×10^{13} Hz; 1.63×10^{-5} m
10. 8.45×10^{14} Hz; 5.60×10^{-19} J
11. 8.923×10^{-7} m; 2.292×10^{-19} J
12. 5.436×10^{16} Hz; 5.519×10^{-9} m

Group II.

1. −314 Kcal/mole
2. For n = 1; $E_n = -313.6$ Kcal/mole
   For n = 2; $E_n = -78.40$ Kcal/mole
   For n = 3; $E_n = -34.84$ Kcal/mole
3. E = 40.9 Kcal/mole
4. E = −58.8 Kcal/mole
5. $f = 1.0 \times 10^{14}$ Hz
6. $E = 2.98 \times 10^{-12}$ ergs
7. 1.79×10^{12} ergs/mole
8. 4.14×10^{14} Hz
9. $r_3 = 9r_0$
10. $\lambda = \dfrac{h}{mc}$

Electrochemistry: pp. 149

1. 54 g of silver
2. 82 g of zinc
3. 0.42 g of aluminum
4. 2.48 A
5. a. +1.02 V; Fe^{3+} (aq) | Fe^{2+} (aq)
   b. +0.46 V; Ag^{+} (aq) | Ag (s)
   c. +1.56 V; Ag^{+} (aq) | Ag (s)
   d. +0.74 V; Cu^{2+} (aq) | Cu (s)
   e. +1.22 V; Br_2^{0} (l) | Br^{-} (aq)
   f. +2.00 V; Cu^{2+} (aq) | Cu (s)
   g. +0.49 V; Ni^{2+} (aq) | Ni (s)
   h. +0.12 V; Co^{2+} (aq) | Co (s)

Index

The following list identifies the locations of exercises and tables for topics included in this book.